Retrospect and Prospect

Retrospect & Prospect

Studies in International Relations
Naval and Political

By

A. T. Mahan, D.C.L., LL.D.

Captain, United States Navy

Author of " The Influence of Sea Power upon History,
1660–1783," " The Influence of Sea Power
upon the French Revolution and
Empire," etc.

KENNIKAT PRESS, INC./PORT WASHINGTON, N. Y.

RETROSPECT AND PROSPECT

First Published in 1902
Reissued in 1968 by Kennikat Press
Library of Congress Catalog Card No: 68- 15831
Manufactured in the United States of America

PREFACE

IN their main features, the following essays are in direct sequence to those of the author's previous volumes, "The Interest of America in Sea Power," and "The Problem of Asia." The title article, Retrospect and Prospect, in its scope serves as a connecting link between the present and their predecessors; indicating the continuity of interest and gradual development of the several subjects dealt with. As the future has passed into the present, it has brought with it the unfolding of inevitable policy, evolving fresh problems, that are in essence only new phases of a steady progression, which in its course is making history.

As has hitherto usually been the case, the articles in this book for the most part have been written, not of the author's own initiative, but in response to the request of editors. Such significance as may attach to this is due to the fact that the work consequently indicates, not

the trend of a single mind, but the outlook of
those whose business is to study the current
of events, to watch the tide of popular interest
and feeling, and thus to provide for readers
information or discussion upon matters toward
which general curiosity is seen to be turning.
It is perfectly consistent with the general tendency thus avouched, and even illustrative of it,
that the series, if it may be called such in virtue of a consecutiveness rather essential than
formal, has led out from considerations narrowly American, with which the papers began,
into the broad field of world policies; for
thither our nation also is indisputably and
irresistibly moving.

Herein lies whatever of lasting value or
interest may attach to the subjects treated, or
the treatment given.   In retrospect, and from
this point of view, it now seems a kind of happy
forecast that the first of the long succession,
written over twelve years ago, began with the
words, " Indications are not wanting of an
approaching change in the thoughts and policy
of Americans as to their relations with the
world outside their own borders." [1]   The pres-
age has been fulfilled, far beyond any consciousness then possible to the writer.

[1] Interest of America in Sea Power, p. 3.

I desire to return my cordial thanks, for the permission here to reprint, to the several proprietors and editors of the periodicals in which the articles first appeared. I owe to them not only the recognition of their courtesy in this respect, but the further acknowledgment that, save for their intervention, probably no single one would have been undertaken. The name of each magazine, with the date of publication, is attached to the title in the Table of Contents. The dates at the head of the articles show the time of writing.

A. T. MAHAN.

SEPTEMBER, 1902.

CONTENTS

I

RETROSPECT AND PROSPECT

RETROSPECT AND PROSPECT

IT has often been remarked, as a curious coincidence, that momentous events, directive of the fortunes of nations and of the world, are found to cluster about the end of our conventional centuries. The final decade of the fifteenth saw both the discovery of America and its complement in maritime achievement, the reaching of India by the passage round the Cape of Good Hope. It witnessed the consummation of the Spanish monarchy by the fall of the last of the Moorish kingdoms, at the very instant that the new possessions in America constituted the commencements of the Spanish Empire. During it occurred also, in 1494, the first of the organized French invasions of Italy, concerning which a master of history has observed that it marked the end of the middle ages, — and so the beginnings of modern history, — because it put forth a scheme of aggrandizement foreign to mediæval conceptions. France and Spain, in rivalry, the scope of which was not yet realized by either, were preparing to attempt the extension of their power over the rest of Europe.

In this effort Spain first succeeded; but, as the sixteenth century drew to its close, the annihilation of the Armada, in 1588, gave resounding proof of her inefficiency as a maritime nation. This defect had for its near result the success of the Dutch in their struggle for independence; but in it was necessarily involved the ultimate downfall of the primacy of Spain among nations, and of her colonial Empire, then apparently untouched. The years remaining to 1600 were spent by her in continued strife with the seamen of England and Holland, the predestined destroyers of her international predominance. To this position France succeeded, reaching the height of her power in the latter half of the seventeenth century; but in 1688 the English Revolution, which decided finally the conflict between King and Parliament, thus shaping the future of another Empire, imparted also the impulse for the descent of France from the eminence she had attained. The coming of William of Orange to the throne entailed as a necessary consequence the accession of England to the two general wars of the Continent against Louis XIV. These, by their drain upon his resources, and the miseries undergone by his kingdom, sapped the foundations of the absolutism upon which the greatness of France had been erected, and precipitated the nation upon the path to decay and revolution.

Great Britain at the same epoch, and through the same causes, was urged further along the way that led her at the end of the war of the Spanish Succession, in 1713, to the unquestioned and unapproached naval supremacy in which lay the germ of her expansion that was to be. Her progress in territorial and commercial aggrandizement was the dominant feature of the eighteenth century, which, though one of chequered strife, was marked upon the whole by the ascent of Great Britain, and still more by the decisive decline of France. As it drew to its close, Louis XVI., in 1788, by summoning the States General to meet after an intermission of many generations, gave the signal for the French Revolution. This, like

its English predecessor, brought France and
Great Britain into a prolonged warfare which
divides into two periods, the Republic and the
Empire, corresponding to the last two wars
of Louis XIV. At the peace of 1815 Great
Britain stood in influence at the head of the
states of European civilization, with a secured
colonial empire, which, in the final decade of
the century, has involved her in a war the most
momentous she has known since Waterloo,
and probably productive of permanent results
to her imperial constitution.

More striking outwardly, even if not more
actually decisive, were other events that occurred between 1890 and 1900. The disap-
pearance of the colonial empire of Spain after
four hundred years of continuous life, although
but the close of a long process of decline, had
singular dramatic effect. The once colossal
structure that so long was crumbling had yet
retained a phantom grandeur, a relic of real
greatness, which enhanced the majesty of the
final fall; for in the days of her supremacy
Spain had over England an ascendency which
France never attained, and the vastness of her
power made upon the imagination of English-

men of that day an impression, traces of which long remained and have been transmitted to their descendants in the United States. In history, too, few events have been told us with as great narrative force as the conquest of Granada, and the early contact of Spain with America. Upon them the genius of American writers has dwelt with peculiar sympathy, both from their intrinsic romantic interest and their close connection with the beginnings of our own country. In her past, thus told, Spain has an immortality resembling that of Rome; and like her she survives and ever will survive in the tales of her heroic prime, and in the enduring impress of her speech and national characteristics left upon great part of the peoples of the new world.

The loss of Cuba, Porto Rico, and the Philippines, the last remnants of a former vast dominion, is an event which, so far as Spain is involved, concerns the past only. At most, if it has for her a future, it is one as yet not even vaguely indicated. As a matter of world interests, its effect upon her is part of the retrospect. From the same point of view the future of that catastrophe lies in the influence it is to exert upon the prospective course of the United States, upon her internal constitutional development and her external policy. Not only in the lost possessions of Spain has the old order yielded, giving place to the new. To the former mother country, forced back upon herself, to seek in the organization of her abundant internal resources the spring of a new life, it may yet prove a cause of national regeneration, the precursor of re-entrance at some future day upon international power resting on more solid foundations. Upon the United States it has imposed the necessity of reconsidering some of the postulates that were supposed fundamental and irreversible in the scheme of her national existence, and of her international relations. The Bible of American political tradition has had new light thrown upon it, and has had to submit to new criticism, based upon truths newly apprehended under the pressure of unforeseen conditions. It would not be unprecedented that popular conception of the meaning of ideas and phrases, formulated and transmitted by our ancestors, should be found imperfect or exaggerated under the clearer appreciation of a later day. The authority hitherto attaching to the popular understanding may in such case have to be transferred to the correcter signification which advancing experience shall have revealed; and obligation, true obedience, will then be seen due to the spirit not to the letter. This would be but the repetition of a very old story in the political as in the religious history of mankind. Whenever it happens, however, the transition of thought and action consequent upon such riper views affects both inner principle and outward action. It must therefore bring shock to those who are too old to change; and when compressed within a very few years, as our recent experience has been, the blow is not broken by the slow reconcilement which successive steps effect. It is not surprising that the recoil on the part of those thus dismayed has been intense, and, it must be added, marked less by reasonableness of argument than by extravagance of expression; by tenacious insistence upon the traditional letter and stubborn rejection of evident modifying circumstance.

Yet, although in point of duration of time the change has been too sudden, or at least too rapid, to allow the process of gradual

mental adjustment which obviates moral distress, it has not been without its marked successive stages which might have prepared an
attentive onlooker for the final outcome.   I
have been told that at the time of the regeneration of the material of the navy, and the lay-
ing down of modern ships, some fifteen years
ago, a sagacious political student remarked
that the measure would be followed by expansive results resembling those we have recently
witnessed.   There was here, I think, the error
of taking one link in a chain of events for a
final cause; but nevertheless the observer
showed that having a clue in his hand he
could, as they say at sea, " underrun " it, till
it led him to the unseen point at which it for
the moment terminated.   That mysterious
thread of purpose which runs through the
progression of history comes to the surface
from time to time in some marks of evident
preparation.   These may be construed, according to individual bias, either as providential,
or merely as symptomatic of a tendency already
formed, and which unconsciously manifests
itself in particular actions conducive to its
general end. (Whichever view be adopted, the

opportune renewal of the navy is to my apprehension not a cause, but one in a series of events which has constituted the general unwitting advance of the nation towards wider influence. It was the more notable because without visible immediate urgency, save that of repairing a cumulative neglect which had resulted in atrophy. No cloud on the political horizon commanded it; but when the cloud afterwards arose the navy was there.

The foregoing remarks are prefatory to the following brief survey of incidents in our own history, which have impressed upon the final decade of the nineteenth century a significance for us, resembling those noted in its predecessors, prophetic of issues not yet fully to be foreseen. It was undertaken at the request of the editor of the *World's Work*, — not by my own initiative. Thus much is said in explanation of an attempt which of my proper motion would scarcely have been made; for the hasty glance which it caused over my occasional magazine papers, during the ten years in question, gave me an unexpected start as I realized from them the singularly different points of view necessarily occupied by an American, at their beginning and at their end, because of changes only partly foreshadowed at the earlier day when I began to write.

It was in August, 1890, that the editor of the *Atlantic Monthly*, Mr. Horace E. Scudder, wrote to ask from me what proved to be the first magazine article I ever published. He referred to a very brief and casual remark in my book then recently out — " The Influence of Sea Power upon History " — touching the exposed condition of our Pacific Coast in the event of an isthmian canal being made. I had quoted in that connection the expression of a French admiral to me, during a cruise then recent, that in our " little corner " of the world we did not need the military and naval preparation incumbent upon the nations of Europe. To this I added, " Yet should that little corner be invaded by a new commercial route through the isthmus, the United States in her turn may have the rude awakening of those who have abandoned their share in the common birthright of all people — the sea."

This reflection, which followed upon a summary of the consequences to Spain — and, it may be added, to France — of a like neglect, had caught Mr. Scudder's attention, and he wrote to know whether I could give the *Atlantic* a paper upon the following general argument. "The centre of maritime operations has shifted once from the Mediterranean to the Atlantic. It *may* pass in the *distant* future (my italics) to the Pacific. Meanwhile, would not the completion of a canal, taken with the British movements at the terminal of the Canadian Pacific, the occidentalizing of Japan, and the growth of Australasia, immensely quicken the process? and, if so, will not the Pacific Coast of our country become a far more important factor in our historical development than it has been?" It will be observed that Mr. Scudder's suggestion, consciously or unconsciously to himself, transcended the bounds of United States' interests, and embraced in its scope the politics of the world.

The canal as yet is not, though it has very measurably advanced through the tedious stages that precede undertakings the importance of which is rather national than corporate, and which therefore do not find their support in private enterprise; but how much of what is here outlined has passed from the realm of speculation to that of action? and how little distant does that future now appear as compared to the anticipations of 1890? In writing on these themes in those days one felt that, while the chain of reasoning was eminently logical, yet there was a lack of solid foundation; that though argumentation were sound, premise was perhaps mistaken; and that when indulging in such forecasts one was in the fantastic sphere familiarized to us by Mr. Edward Bellamy and others. But what events have since happened, bringing the abstract conceptions of theorists and extremists, as they then seemed, down to earth in very concrete realization! What once were visions are now accepted as solid present matters of course by our very practical nation. They have almost ceased to excite vivid interest, because of a familiarity which eliminates surprise. The condition, however, if no longer novel, is one so substantial that it can never again in our day pass out of sight, or out of national consideration.

Since Mr. Scudder wrote, the occidentalization of Japan, in methods although not in national spirit, — which changes much more slowly, — has been fully demonstrated to an astonished world by the war of 1894 with China. It is one of the incidents of the closing nineteenth century. To this achievement in the military sphere, in the practice of war which Napoleon called the science of barbarians, must be added the development of civil institutions that has resulted in the concession to Japan of all international dignity and privilege; and consequently of a control over the administration of justice among foreigners within her borders, not heretofore obtained by any other Oriental State. It has thus become evident that the weight of Japan in the international balances depends not upon the quality of her achievement, which has been shown to be excellent, but upon the gross amount of her power. Moreover, while in wealth and population, with the resources dependent upon them, she may be deficient, — though rapidly growing, — her geographical position relatively to the Eastern centre of interest, and her advantage of insularity, go far to compensate such defect. These confer upon her as a factor in the Eastern problem an influence resembling

in kind, if not equalling in degree, that which
Great Britain has held and still holds in the
international relations centring around Europe,
the Atlantic, and the Mediterranean.

Yet the change in Japan, significant as it
is and influential upon the great problem of
the Pacific and Asia, is less remarkable and
less important than that which has occurred
in the United States. If in the Orient a
nation may be said to have been born in a day,
even so the event is less sudden and less revo-
lutionary than the conversion of spirit and of
ideals — the new birth — which has come over
our own country. In this are evident a rapidity and a thoroughness which bespeak impulse
from an external source, rather than any conscious set process of deliberation, of self-determination within, such as has been that of Japan
in her recognition and adoption of material
improvements forced upon her attention in
other peoples. No man or group of men can
pretend to have guided and governed our
people in the adoption of a new policy, the
acceptance of which has been rather instinc-
tive — I would prefer to say inspired — than
reasoned. There is just this difference be-

tween Japan and ourselves, the two most
changed of peoples within the last half-century.
She has adopted other methods; we have received another purpose. The one conversion
is material, the other spiritual. When we
talk about expansion we are in the realm of
ideas. The material addition of expansion —
the acreage, if I may so say — is trivial compared with our previous possessions, or with
the annexations by European states within a
few years. The material profit otherwise, the
national gain to us, is at best doubtful. What
the nation has gained in expansion is a regen-
erating idea, an uplifting of the heart, a seed
of future beneficent activity, a going out of
self into the world to communicate the gift it
has so bountifully received.

In this connection, and in emphatic contrast
of past with present, how very apt is the expression of the French admiral, our "little
corner," — the Jack Horner of nations. How
accurately did the phrase then represent our
own estimate, and that of the outer world,
concerning our political and international exposure, responsibilities, and duties, in days
when the ideas, imperialism and anti-imperial-

ism, had scarcely received formulation. I remember that imperialism had not long before been associated in my mind with certain vague impressions of Mr. Blaine and his supposed projects. As far as my own views went, I might say I was up to 1885 traditionally an anti-imperialist; but by 1890 the study of the influence of sea power and its kindred expansive activities upon the destiny of nations had converted me, and my new faiths, thus originated, colored the first of my writings, as they have continued to do the rest.

The natural tendency of the line of thought which leads up to the appreciation of sea power and to the vision of expansion of national influences — rather than of national possessions — when acting upon a person inheriting Anglo-Saxon political traditions, is in commercial matters towards freedom of trade. Mr. Blaine, a protectionist by antecedents and by party affiliation, as his mind expanded to embrace the idea of an American system, inevitably moved on to modify the idea of protection to that of reciprocity. Reciprocity is far from being free trade; but in principle it is nearer to that than to protection. Reciprocity has abandoned the view-point of exclusive interest, which is the citadel of protection, to embrace that of mutual benefit, the cornerstone upon which the advocates of freedom of trade rest their argument.

The beneficiaries of protection see this clearly enough, as is shown by their recent capture of the Reciprocity Convention and renewed proclamation of their favorite dogma. The fate of the measures proposed for Cuban relief, in the session that has passed since this article was first written, is probably an indication in the same direction. But protection is essentially a defensive measure, and in all struggles, in commerce as in war, it is not defensive action but offensive — conquest, expansion — which ultimately wins. It is in truth this factor of offence, shown in the activity of the American mind, in the energy with which it carries ideas into practice and in the flexibility which readily embraces improvement, that has won the superiority which enables us latterly to invade the markets of the world. The credit is claimed for protection, and is too easily yielded because the coincidence of our advance with the protective system confuses thought; but it is easy to see that, left to itself alone, the assurance of an adequate market — the secured home market — removes that necessity which is the mother of invention, the necessity which competition imposes. American inventive aptitude and American energy have triumphed over the enervating influence of the protection that would and long did restrain them from efficient action without their own borders, and in so doing hindered that development of sea power, commercial and naval, which expansion, material and moral, requires. Reciprocity, increased freedom of movement, is the logical corollary of expansion, which itself is but increase of scope and power to act.

It is, therefore, not a disconnected feature of the situation that reciprocity is no longer the idea of the few, but has assumed a conspicuous place in the thought of a party and of a leader — President McKinley — whose very names have been synonymous with protection. It is but another aspect of that mysterious, subtle influence, already vaguely felt in the early years of the last decade of the nineteenth century, and then, before its end, bursting suddenly into life and taking definite form in the acceptance of national expansion — territorial, political, naval, commercial. In every one of these aspects we find not merely development, but extension; not merely growth from what has been, but the grafting on of that which before found no place in our national conceptions. It resembles the breach of continuity between the middle ages and modern times. Our development on former lines has reached into maturity and, unless renewed by fresh influence, would pass into decadence; that which now succeeds it is new life, not new growth. In the Philippines, Porto Rico, and Hawaii, we have territorial expansion. They, as well as Cuba, require us to constitute and establish political relations of a kind not heretofore admitted as compatible with our scheme of existence, — in short, expansion of political thought. These changed conditions have necessarily entailed naval expansion; and there can be little doubt that they will also imperceptibly — perhaps the protectionist may say "insidiously" — promote reciprocity of trade, expansion of commercial thought, with the logical consequences that follow the admission of a new principle.

Mr. Scudder named my first article, " The United States Looking Outward." It was particularly apt, for it exactly described the national attitude then. We were looking, but we had not got beyond that point where a baby vaguely follows with its eyes something which has caught its attention but not entered its understanding. Yet I have felt it significant, then and now, that in casting round for a start- ing point I, with all my professional prepossessions naturally maritime and military, should have opened my theme, not by a discussion of the naval or strategic situation, but by indicat- ing the essential feebleness of a commercial policy which was primarily — nay wholly — de- fensive, and in which aggression, expansion, found no place. I quoted joyfully Mr. Blaine's words, " It is not an ambitious destiny for so great a country to manufacture only what we can consume, or produce only what we can eat;" and I had pleasure in likening the ex- travagances of the then recent tariff legislation to Napoleon's Continental system, — a proph- ecy by implication which it must be admitted has not yet received fulfilment.

There has, however, been realized so much of

the other indications of the future in that article, so much beyond what I dared to expect in my time, that I am not without hope that herein also I may live to see beneficial results. This paper some half-dozen years later was gathered into a book with a series of seven others on kindred topics, all falling under the general head of arguments for expansion; not, indeed, specific in detail, but I think not without clearness in the enunciation of principles governing its general direction and character. The very enumeration of the successive titles has particular suggestion to those interested in the general subject, as bearing upon the gradual expansion of the nation's thought, the gradual, though very rapid, development of policy; because in none save one, and that the last of all, was the article prompted by myself. In each case, as in the first, it was elicited by the request of the editors, whose perceptions were quickened by their need to watch the trend of events and provide the public with matter concerning which its interest was stirring.

Of course, naval officers, moving round the world, talking with its inhabitants in various

localities and afterward bringing the various
ideas to the common exchange of the mess-
table and of other professional intercourse,
imbibe a good deal of information particularly
pertinent to the question of expansion, needing
only digestion and arrangement to have a usefulness quite peculiar to itself. I was therefore pretty full of matter, and to this day
remember the delightful ease of production
due to that fact, as contrasted with some heart-
breaking work done since. Nevertheless, for
the reasons noted, the record of articles traces
not my development, but the progress of national awakening from 1890 to 1897; to the
eve, that is, of the great year when old things
passed away, and all things became new in the
birth of a new national resolve, quickened into
life by the crash of a falling empire and the
devolution of its responsibilities upon our conscience. In some measure through the circumstances of my profession, but chiefly
through the solicitation of others, it fell to me,
though by no means to me alone, to chronicle
from time to time the stages of the antecedent
process of preparation; to note the advance of
ideas, as step by step the editorial watchers saw

that advance had been made, but needed definition and formulation.

As far as known to me, " The United States Looking Outward " attracted no special attention in any quarter. The only comment I can now recall was by, I think, a Protectionist sheet, to the effect that it seemed to be an argument for free trade. This critic apparently had not got beyond the first two pages. Yet the other topics, incidentally touched or more fully developed, need only to be named in order to show the most casual reader of to-day the important possibilities involved in the external objects which demanded the consideration of the United States in 1890. Samoa; Hawaii; German commercial and colonial push in the Caroline and other islands near the Philippines, which the empire has since acquired by purchase; the progress of German influence in Central and South America, notably in the southern province of Brazil; the increasing importance of the Pacific and the effects upon it of an isthmian canal ; the political wisdom of maintaining with Great Britain a cordial understanding, approaching coöperation, though distinctly rejecting the idea of alliance; the

question of purchase by European powers of
stations in the West Indies, such as the Danish
St. Thomas and the Dutch Curaçao; the
strategic features of the Gulf of Mexico and
the Caribbean Sea, with the transcendent military value of Cuba and Jamaica in that connection. As regards these external points the
United States was perhaps looking outward,
but she evidently was not, as a nation, taking
notice; and my remarks that "whether they
will or no, Americans must now begin to look
outwards," rested upon the necessities of the
case as set forth, not upon any certain evidence
of such watchfulness begun.

The first really arousing event occurred
where naval officers had long recognized the
most critical of our external interests; the one
where political change of condition detrimen-
tal to our military security was most likely to
occur, and to be allowed by default. The
islands and mainland of America were fairly
covered from serious aggression by national
susceptibility, pointed in the phrase " the
Monroe Doctrine." What the doctrine was,
was perhaps not very clearly understood, but it
was a good war-cry and might be depended on

to serve its turn, although the experience of generations had shown it impotent to insure naval expansion adequate to enforce its assertion. Hawaii, however, could not be construed to fall under the Monroe Doctrine; and, although many men in the country appreciated its consequence to us, it was not certain that the people generally would sustain an active policy based upon the need of our predominance there.

It is not necessary to recall in detail the occurrences in Hawaii at the end of 1892, which led to the treaty of annexation sent to the Senate by President Harrison, and withdrawn upon the change of administration by President Cleveland. What then occurred was the outcome of conditions which had led me in my first article to say, " At this moment internal troubles are imminent in the Sandwich Islands, where it should be our fixed determination to allow no foreign influence to equal our own." The submittal and withdrawal of the treaty in rapid succession demonstrated the doubtful attitude of national opinion in 1893, just as the annexation of five years later showed, not growth, but conversion. Nevertheless I have always felt the first abortive movement to have been the more conspicuous landmark. Though without result, it was the awakening; too late to seize the current opportunity, but not so late as to be unprepared for the events which the near future was to bring.

It may profitably be noted that the contrary decisions of the two administrations in this matter were prophetic of party fortunes. In the face of an emergency such as in 1893 arose in Hawaii, with its extravagantly mixed population, foreign not only in extraction, but in sentiment and allegiance, a political party which held that our action was to be controlled by a count of heads among them was evidently unable to deal with impending questions. I do not pretend to have foreseen the events that ensued between 1893 and 1898; but it was clear enough in 1892 that we had to look out into the Pacific and toward China. We could never act there efficiently with our intellects manacled by a traditionalism which saw in the population of Hawaii a capacity for self-determination like that of the Pilgrims, and which failed to comprehend that Hawaii was an outpost of the utmost value in the Pacific, for the tenure of which, in the rapid decay of the aboriginal population, East and West were already striving.

This Hawaiian business drew from me, by request from the *Forum*, of which Mr. Walter H. Page was then editor, my second article, " Hawaii and Our Sea Power ; " to which succeeded almost immediately an invitation from the *Atlantic* to treat the question of the isthmus and its canal from the same point of view. The latter of itself, coming so quickly, indicates how the former affair had waked the people up, not to Hawaii alone, but to the broader issues of which Hawaii only happened by special circumstances to become the exponent. I do not think I erred then in saying, in the first of these articles, with reference to Mr. Harrison's treaty, " The United States now finds herself compelled to answer a question — to make a decision — not unlike and not less momentous than that required of the Roman Senate when the Mamertine garrison invited it to occupy Messina, and so to abandon the hitherto traditional policy which had confined the expansion of Rome to the Italian peninsula." " What is here involved is not so much a particular action as a principle pregnant of great consequences."

A reasonable regard for the patience of readers, and for the proprieties, limits me to mentioning simply the titles of the articles asked from me in the successive years 1894, 1895, 1896, 1897; indicative not only in their particular subject, but in the very order of the series, of the awakening consciousness of the people, reflected in the attentive minds of editors. They were, " The Possibilities of Anglo-American Reunion," " The Future in Relation to American Naval Power," " Preparedness for Naval War," and " A Twentieth Century Outlook."

The last decade of the century carried the outward look on from the Isthmus and Hawaii, and from the naval preparations essential to maintaining the nation's requirements, as formulated in the Monroe Doctrine and evident in the conditions of the Pacific, to consider the general outward movement of the European world, evinced in the new era of colonization and the search for naval stations which had recently begun. This impulse, I believe, will hereafter be recognized as the chief among those transmitted by the nineteenth century to its successor. Viewed with the new and significant restlessness among the Oriental peoples, aroused at length, by intimate contact with Europeans, from the torpor and change-lessness of ages — an awakening of which the occidentalizing of Japan is merely the most conspicuous incident — this is the significant feature of the opening century, that should direct the attention of our people in external policy. This European movement has three principal fields: the Levant, — in which Egypt may for convenience be included, — Africa, and Asia. Though locally Asiatic, the Levant is a European interest, pure and simple; and Africa, in relation to world politics, is but an annex of Europe, geographically as well as, now, by pre-emption. Eastern Asia, however, and China especially, with all its immense possibilities, stands over against us, demanding our most careful and constant thought; all the more because there would appear to be a disposition in some quarters to question our right of inter-est. In a Parliamentary blue book published some eighteen months ago with reference to the incipient troubles in China which afterward became so acute, the Russian ambassador at Peking is mentioned as saying to his British colleague that only Russia and Great Britain had serious interests in China. We shall not err greatly, I imagine, in believing that Great Britain does not share this sentiment.

As a matter of national decision Hawaii is already past history, and the Monroe Doctrine seems even now to be approaching a condition of general silent acquiescence, which, if realized, will give to it also the quality of permanence that distinguishes the past from the present. The living external issue of the present and the future, the field for us alive with multifold possibilities and uncertainties, is Eastern Asia; so far in 1901 have we travelled, in the eight years that began by seeing even Hawaii rejected and have ended with the Philippines possessed. The elements of the situation in China, as determinative of national watchfulness, may be stated as follows. The great stream and valley of the Yangtse Kiang is the natural focus of trade for the greater and richer part of the empire, which it divides roughly into two halves. It is navigable continuously by steamers for a thousand miles, and for a great part of that distance

by sea-going vessels, including large ships of
war.   Here, therefore, is the great commanding interest of commercial nations and of maritime Powers.   Here, and here only, apart from
the seaboard itself, can they effectually assert
their force to control infringement upon China's
right of self-direction, and to support the
Chinese themselves in their resistance which,
unaided, has not been able to retain Manchuria.
The maritime Powers are several; but of them
France has seen fit to identify her policy with
Russia and cannot be depended upon, even if
her irritable national sensitiveness permitted
other peoples to count upon the reasonableness
of her action in any particular case.   Regard
for the interests of China, of the commercial
world at large, and of our own people, therefore impel us to coöperation with Great Britain, the greatest of naval states; for her aim, as
a free-trade nation with large carrying trade,
must necessarily be to increase the volume of
commerce in a country like China, and to support her against the encroachments of another
people, of whose policy exclusive trade is a
dominant factor.   For the same reasons, though
to a less degree, we find ourselves impelled to

act in this matter in unison with Germany and Japan. As the world is now balanced, the British Empire is in external matters our natural though not our formal ally.

The canal, Hawaii, and the Philippines are valuable to us as positions even more than as possessions. In the problem of Eastern Asia, still in an early stage of its solution and of doubtful issue, they are important as facilitating our access to the seas of China and to the valley of the Yangtse, and as furnishing territorial support to our action there. Intrinsically, their future now presents but few elements of anxiety. In the grave uncertainties surrounding China, it is along the great river, of which Shanghai is the chief port, that the interest of the western world centres. From it our eyes should never wander. There rests the centre of Chinese power as susceptible of future development, and there it should receive firm support from us, disregardful of the place where the Chinese Court may see fit to establish its abode. Peking, as has been clearly shown, is too easily controlled from the land side. Partition is one thing which we may well reject; but it would be very different to see established along the course of the Yangtse a native Power strong enough to resist dictation from the capital, and, if need be, strong enough also to resist those by whom the capital may be oppressed.

CONDITIONS DETERMINING THE NAVAL EXPANSION OF THE UNITED STATES

CONDITIONS DETERMINING THE NAVAL EXPANSION OF THE UNITED STATES

January, 1902.

A T this time, while naval manœuvres are attracting attention among the people of the United States, it is pertinent to point out that it is commonly, but mistakenly, supposed that the present necessity for naval enlargement rests upon the acquisition of oversea territories, as a consequence of the war with Spain. The error is natural, for undoubtedly the war convinced the American people of the advantage — nay, the necessity — of a great navy, and so led to the increase we are witnessing; but the necessity was approaching unobserved, and would have come upon the nation unawares and unprepared, but for the fortunate intervention of the war, and its demonstration of the usefulness of navies.

We have the highest military authority for saying that the best and only sure form of de-

fence is to take the offensive, or at least to be
evidently ready so to do at brief notice. The
navy is essentially and pre-eminently a force
that thus acts, in virtue of the mobility which
is its prime quality; and it is scarcely necessary to argue that the more wide-spread the
interests open to attack, the more valuable in
this sense the navy is, and the more numerous
and powerful must it be. So long as the
United States had no external possessions, it
was comparatively easy to blind people to the
usefulness of a navy, or to the necessity for it.
A navy for coast defence only was then a plausible, though deceitful, cry; and it was a very
easy further step to say that fortifications, sta-
tionary land defences, were cheaper and more
effective. On the narrow ground of passive
defence, that is true; therefore, ignorance of
military principles being characteristic of mankind generally, and of Americans perhaps particularly, the need of a mobile force to act
offensively could not obtain recognition.

It is not the least of the advantages derived
from the new possessions that this condition of
the public mind can exist no longer. It was

very soundly argued, by the American opponents of the expansion which has been realized in the last decade of the nineteenth century, that transmarine acquisitions would be so many new exposed points, to be supported by sea only, not by land, as the continental territory can. They were very right, and this is very true; the flaw in their argument, as well as the beam in the eye of the American public, which prevented it from seeing clearly, was the failure to note that, even when not possessing a square foot of territory without its borders, there were manifold interests abroad, assailable by a superior navy, and only to be protected by such display of force as should make it not worth while to arouse the nation to action.

The argument of the opponents of territorial expansion, even within moderate limits, and with due regard to locality and consequent utility in the positions acquired, was thus plausible, and was deplorably successful; but it was fallacious. It adduced a sound military reason, — the increased exposure, — but wholly ignored qualifying considerations of the most serious character, reversive of conclusions. It may with much more certainty be now alleged, and the assertion can be supported to the point of demonstration, that the acquisitions of recent years, despite the additional requirement of their defence imposed upon the United States, have not necessitated any increase of naval force beyond that which would have been imperatively demanded at the present time, had they never passed into American hands. More still, they have lessened the burden of purely naval increase, which but for them would have been necessary ; for by the tenure of them, and due development of their resources, the navy itself receives an accession of strength, an augmented facility of movement, by resting upon strong positions for equipment and repair, — upon bases, to use the military term, — in several parts of the world where national interests demand naval protection of the kind already mentioned; namely, readiness to take the offensive instantly.

Facilities of this character add a percentage of value to a given mobile force, military or naval, for they by so much increase its power and its mobility. This percentage may be difficult of precise definition as to amount, but it none the less exists. That coal can be obtained near at hand, plentifully, and with certainty; that ships can remain in readiness, and in security, near the possible scene of operations; that they can be repaired there, instead of returning to the United States; all these conditions, which the new possessions will afford, enable the work on the spot to be done by fewer ships. Furthermore, by their storage facilities, by their accumulated and natural resources, they diminish the immediate dependence upon home by a long chain of communications, which is the great drain on all military operations.

Thus, according to the particular conditions, one ship may do the work of two, or three ships of five, or perhaps nine of ten; but, be the proportion more or less, the gain in efficiency means, as such gain always does, smaller numbers and therefore less expense. When a battleship in war time runs upon an uncharted rock, as the *Oregon* did a year ago in the China Seas, it makes an immense difference to an admiral, and to the operations in hand, whether she can be repaired at a distance of five hundred miles, or of five thousand.   The case is the same with minor repairs, and with the renewal of coal, one of the greatest of naval anxieties.   For instance, it would be difficult to exaggerate the value of Guantanamo, only fifty miles from Santiago de Cuba, to the American fleet off the latter port, which otherwise had to coal in the open, or depend upon a base many hundred miles away.

It may be advisable here to notice passingly an argument at times maintained, and often advanced during recent discussions concerning the annexation of the Philippines, that, while such bases of naval action are intrinsically advantageous, there attaches to them no expediency of holding adjacent territory in political tenure.   The United States therefore, so it was urged, for the security of her naval situation in eastern waters would require in the Philippines no more than a navy yard.   From the military point of view this is wholly inaccurate.   Any military permanent station, land fortress or naval arsenal, gains immeasurably in strength from the support of a friendly region in which it is situated, because of the contribution to its resources and the distance at which attack is held.   The impressiveness of the word "isolation," which we all instinctively feel, testifies to this condition. Nor is it conclusive against the military argument that the friendliness be of a passive or reluctant character, as of a population subjected to military control. This consideration is indeed material to the general conduct of a war, for the force thus engaged in insuring submission is withdrawn from that available for other operations; but so long as it is effective in compelling or inducing the co-operation of the inhabitants, either as peaceful workmen and agriculturists, or more positively in the field, the particular fortress, land or sea, is far stronger than it could be if surrounded by territory under alien government, even though neutral.

Extent of territory is a real factor in military strength, and for this reason a small island is decisively less valuable than a large one. It is a distinct weakness to Gibraltar that it is backed by a country wholly foreign, though probably not belligerent; and Malta, if severed from a predominant navy, would find its intrinsic power inadequate to prolonged endurance. On the other hand, places on the coast of the United States, or of Australia, or New Zealand, though individually weak from a purely military standpoint, derive great increase of resistant force, and still more of productive energy, — a large element in military offensive efficiency, — because in the midst of a friendly and industrious community. The questions of resources and of support, both very important factors in military vigor, turn largely upon this one consideration.

This is not, in itself, an argument for large annexations, or indefinite territorial expansion. These, if desirable, rest upon reasons other than military. We are dealing here with a purely military consideration, and supporting it by military argument, which, however, cannot be pressed to the extent of supporting an action political in origin. The military argument amounts simply to this: that a moderate number of such bases, suitably chosen in view of their position and resources, strengthen a military or naval situation, and thereby enable fewer men or fewer ships to do the necessary work; but it must be at once qualified by the other perfectly familiar military maxim, that the multiplication of such bases, as soon as you pass the limits of reasonable necessity, becomes a source of weakness, multiplying exposed points, and entailing division of force. It is not even a matter of indifference that you have too many; it is a positive injury. Consequently, the necessity of naval bases to efficient naval action cannot by itself be made into an argument for indefinite expansion.

Such oversea expansion as the United States has so far made has not been primarily for military purposes. Incidentally, it has contributed to naval power, and it has not as yet transcended the limit of utility to that end. What has been already gained is useful, either directly or indirectly; the increase of exposure, as yet, does not equal the increase in strength. It is, of course, very possible that considerations of political or commercial expediency, or even necessity, might lead to acquisitions, the exposure and burden of which would find no compensation in increase of naval strength, or of general national military security. The justification of such measures, if taken, must rest on other than military or naval reasons, and would not concern this argument;

but in fact no such undue expansion has yet occurred.

The march of events, not in the United States only, but over the world at large, not of military or naval events chiefly, but of political events, events economical and commercial, has brought about a necessity for large navies; for navies much increased over the standard of twenty years ago. This is now universally recognized. Of this course of events in those two decades, and their result to-day, the war with Spain, which led directly or indirectly to the acquisition of every foot of insular territory possessed by the United States, is simply one incident; and that an incident rather disconnected, something of a side issue, though one most timely for the welfare of the nation.

Had that war not occurred, there is no reason to believe that the mighty events which have transpired in Africa, Egypt, the Levant, and China, would not have happened; still less that there would not have been the immense commercial developments, which, if less striking, are even more momentous, and more influential at this moment upon the policy of nations. Issues and conditions which are mov-

ing the world would have been as they are had
the distress of Cuba never compelled intervention. The difference now would have been that
the United States would be without Porto Rico,
Hawaii, and the Philippines; without reserved
rights in Cuba, the key of the West Indies and
Gulf of Mexico; and that she would not have
received the impulse, which the war and its
consequent acquisitions most timely gave, to the
building of the navy towards a point necessary
to meet the demands of a political and commercial future, which in any case would have
arrived, and, but for that war, have found the
nation unprepared.

The general strenuous impulse of the great
civilized states of the world, to find and to establish markets and commercial relations outside
their own borders and their own people, has
led to multifold annexations, and to commercial and naval aggressions. In these the United
States has had no part, but they have constituted a political situation that immensely increases her political and commercial anxieties,
and consequently her naval responsibilities;
for, as interests of this kind are outside the
North American continent, it is upon the navy

that their support rests. This external impulse of the commercial nations is of two-fold character. First, there is the perfectly legitimate and unobjectionable form of commercial competition, in open field and without favor; but there is, besides, the effort to extend and sustain commercial advantage by the extension of political power, either by controlling influence or by actual annexation, under cover of either of which the commercial system of the particular country obtains favored conditions, injurious to others, from special privilege all the way up to a practically exclusive market. The history of the past twenty or thirty years abounds in such instances, reversive of the course of trade, even to the destruction at times of a well-established commerce.

Much of this politico-commercial movement has occurred in regions where the United States has been compelled, by her recognized traditional policy, to abstain from intervention, or even remonstrance. The politics are none of our business, and the resultant commercial inconvenience, if it touch us, has to be accepted. This applies to Europe generally; to Africa, which, both by position and now by annexation, is an appendage of Europe; and probably also to those parts of Asia commonly known as the Levant, which by juxtaposition are European in interest. The case is very different in South America, in Eastern Asia, and in the Pacific. From interest in none of these is the United States excluded by the Monroe Doctrine and its corollaries, by which she simply defines her policy to be hands-off in matters of purely European concern; while by express declaration political interference in South America, of a character to intrude European political control, will be resented as directly injurious to American security.

As regards the Pacific and China, the movement there, and especially in the latter, has been lately so much before the public that it is unnecessary to recall details. It is obvious, however, that where the commercial interests at stake are so great, and political conditions so uncertain, the desire to secure commercial opportunity will lead countries that possess force into a dangerous temptation to use it for the extension of their influence. Therefore, unless prepared to maintain the national rights, either singly or in combination with others, backed by force at hand, the United States may find her people excluded, more or less, by the encroachment of rivals.

The case in South America is even more serious; for political interference there not only may injure the nation commercially, but would certainly dishonor it, in face of its clearly avowed policy. It must be remembered that this extension of commerce by political pressure is a leading element in the spirit of the times; and, when such a spirit is looking watchfully for a field in which to act, one so fruitful and so promising as South America can secure exemption only by a display of power to resist, which South America itself does not possess, and which the United States alone can supply.

These are among the leading conditions which necessitate the creation of a powerful navy by the United States, and they are quite independent of her relatively small external possessions, most valuable though these are from the naval point of view. She is confronted, in short, by a general movement of the nations resting upon a spirit spread among their peoples, which seeks to secure commercial advantages in all quarters of the world; peaceably, if may be, but, if not, by pressure. In this collision of interests, force will have a determining part, as it has in all periods of the world's history; and force, in such remote localities, means necessarily naval force. It is upon the spread of this spirit and the action ensuing from it, that the necessity for a great navy rests, and not upon the fact of having assumed oversea charges. Porto Rico, Hawaii, the Philippines, and if there be any other acquisition at present, have not created the necessity; on the contrary, they have reduced the weight of the burden, by contributing to support it.

THE INFLUENCE OF THE SOUTH AFRICAN WAR UPON THE PRESTIGE OF THE BRITISH EMPIRE

THE INFLUENCE OF THE SOUTH AFRICAN WAR UPON THE PRESTIGE OF THE BRITISH EMPIRE

November, 1901.

WITHOUT seeking excessive refinement in definition, it may profitably be recalled that the common colloquial use of the word "prestige" overlooks its primary signification, which involves the idea of illusion, or even of delusion. When employing it in ordinary speech we do not think of a veil concealing truth, but of a solid basis of achievement or power which underlies present acknowledged reputation. Thus the word is practically affirmative, not negative; it suggests actuality, not a mask. But for the very reason that prestige is popular impression, resting upon surface appearance assumed to be substantial fact, it is among the most uncertain of possessions; upon a pedestal to-day, in the dust to-morrow, with the facile fickleness noted in populaces. When to this source of error in the adoption of opinion is added the misguiding influence of strong prejudices, when misunderstanding of conditions combines with bias of judgment, mutabilities of prestige may be both sudden and extreme. " Presto! Change !" and prestidigitator, are prominent and characteristic members of the volatile family to which prestige owes its birth.   The decline of prestige may involve as much illusion as its growth; therefore its value, while not to be denied, may easily be exaggerated.

Prestige then does not necessarily correspond with fact, even moderately; on the contrary, it is apt to be much in excess or much in defect.   Nevertheless, it is a valuable possession; an asset which counts for a good deal in the reckoning of international balances. Accepted at its face value, and repeated in the street from man to man, it constitutes a mass of impression which finally affects even the more judicious and better-informed, and may become of weight in diplomatic action.   Consequently, when impaired, it is worth the effort to restore it, and to bring it into conformity with material facts.   These do not change either with the suddenness, or in the degree, to which mere moral effect is specially liable.

Qualifying the word and its idea with the remarks so far made, the prestige of the British Empire has assuredly suffered diminution from the South African war. Men in the street, and the hurried writers of the press, have received an impression of bafflement, or even of failure, in holding which they support one another. From the very outset prepossession stood ready upon the Continent, and among many of the American people, not only to rejoice over British reverses, but to draw from them quick, disparaging conclusions, affecting prestige, by the easy process of forgetting fundamental conditions and dwelling upon surface events. Precisely the same disposition was entertained towards the United States a year before, at the beginning of our war with Spain, as I had opportunity to observe by the experience of dining in company with several diplomats in a European capital at the moment of the outbreak of hostilities. That the gratification of gloating over our defeats was confidently anticipated also is a matter of common notoriety. We were out of favor, and our

prestige was naturally low. The fortunate
event of our war having at least not lowered
it further, there is no necessity to inquire how
far the original estimate corresponded with the
facts. Of one thing, however, we may be sure;
that had temporary unsuccess attended us, the
difficulties of our undertaking, which formed the
basis of unfavorable prediction and were by no
means small to a dispassionate judgment, would
not in the least have qualified unfavorable criticism. Prejudice is a two-edged sword, and
cuts both ways. So it has been in South
Africa. The evident military difficulties gave
hostile sentiment the basis on which to build
prophecies of disaster; but having served that
purpose, when it comes to comment and inference, the difficulties no longer find place for
consideration.

The military conditions before and during
the war, and now existing in South Africa, are
so much matters of present remembrance that
it is unnecessary to enumerate them at large.
What can profitably be done is to select from
them those which constitute the distinctive
characteristics, differentiating this from other
struggles, and yet at the same time enabling it

to be in some measure classified; for such features suggest resemblances as well as differences. The prominent facts, thus separated from less noteworthy surroundings, can then be brought to the test of criticism as to their positive influence in the present case, and also to comparison with other historical experiences. Whatever may be the prestige, in the strict sense of the word, of the British Empire, at home or abroad, its real meed of praise or blame depends upon the way it has met, and is meeting, these distinctive conditions.

The characteristic elements of this war resulting from the permanent conditions, irrespective of the conduct of the present hostilities, and anterior to their beginning, are (1) The remoteness of the British base of operations from the scene of fighting, contrasted with the nearness of the Boers; in other words, the length of the British lines of communication. (2) The nature and extent of the country over which operations had to be conducted. (3) The character of the hostile people; including therein the advantage which familiarity with a region and its conditions, especially when sparsely settled, undeveloped, and consequently imperfectly known, always gives to inhabitants over invaders. All three particulars, indeed, fall under the general head of communications, which, on the strategic side at least, dominate war. The nature and extent of the country affect materially the maintenance of communications, their security and their rapidity. So also the native and acquired characteristics of the enemy act and react upon communications. If of extremely simple wants, capable of rapid movement, familiar with the country, surrounded by sympathizers, their own communications are relatively invulnerable, and to the same degree they are facilitated in attacking those of the invader. *Rôles* are, in a measure, reversed; the offence is constantly on the defence for his communications, the defence on the offensive against them.

These factors, onerously adverse to Great Britain, were and are permanent. To them must be added a present consideration, which existed from the beginning, but which it was then perhaps impossible to anticipate; namely, the difficulty under which the British Government would be placed in dealing with partially organized forces maintaining insurrection rather

than war; with no organic social system behind them, and, from that very lack, without
vital centres, or social articulations, at which
to strike; capable of indefinite subdivision and
consequent elusiveness, due to the very low
type of social and political cohesion which has
been characteristic of the Boer peoples from
their beginnings. When highly organized and
complex, national vitality may be paralyzed
without killing men; but where organization
is defective, the same end cannot be quickly
reached without a slaughter of individuals from
which modern humanity rightfully revolts.

Here has been the difficulty confronting the
Empire since the end of the war proper. From
the delay in solving it proceeds the present
impairment of prestige, which, granting the
idea of illusion inseparable from the word, is
natural and to be expected. For many obvious
reasons, the individual Boer, when caught, cannot be killed. Great Britain is limited to capture and exportation; processes indefinitely
tedious, owing to the nature of the country
and other causes before noticed, and further
protracted by the necessity of diverting a huge
fraction of the large available forces to the

protection of the communications. These
stretch a thousand miles from the sea-board to
the seat of war, and thence ramify throughout
the extensive regions over which desultory and
elusive fighting may spread. This burden is
even greater than during regular hostilities,
both because the lines are more disseminated,
and because the evasive action of the small
bands now in the field is harder to counteract
than the efforts of large masses, compelled by
their very size to consider their own communications.

The military operations of the war in South
Africa may be divided into two principal and
easily recognized stages. There is, first, that
of regular hostilities, which terminated not long
after the fall of Pretoria; to which succeeded
the existing conditions of what is commonly
called guerilla warfare. In the former, the
British were confronted by large numbers,
more or less organized, acting in masses, and
representing a regular Government which had
its staff of officials and local habitat. In the
present embarrassing situation, the permanent
natural factors (the nature of the country, and
the racial characteristics of the opponents, with

their consequent individual tendencies of action) remain much the same; but the accidental temporary elements are changed. The Boer forces are no longer organized, in the sense of having a common centre of action, or a regular gradation of even military authority. They no longer act in masses, but are scattered in small bodies, much of whose immunity depends upon their faculty of melting away and subsequently reuniting; and there is behind them no recognized and efficient civil government. On the civil side the Boer bands represent a past, not a present; the organic society and government no longer exist.

The conduct of the earlier stage of the war by the British, with its effect upon prestige, is first to be considered. Bearing in mind the respective distances of the antagonists from the seat of war, the outbreak of hostilities gave to the Boers the advantage, to the British the disadvantage, of a surprise. That this is so is seen by considering how the case would have stood had the British Islands been where Cape Colony is. That larger organized forces were not assembled in South Africa at an early date will be differently criticised even by impartial observers. It may at least be observed that, if injurious to the prestige of the Government on the score of unwise delay, it cannot at the same time be attributed to eagerness for war. Also, however viewed, this is chargeable to political calculation, not to military inefficiency. But when war was at last resolved, it cannot, I think, be considered as less than admirable that over 165,000 men, with the vast mass of warlike equipment, were transferred six thousand miles from the British Islands to South Africa in six months. Nor yet that, from the sea-coast, the same huge numbers and equipment were carried by single track railroads a thousand miles inland, there maintained, and within eight months, not of their arrival in Africa, but of their earliest departure from England, had possession of the capitals of both their opponents, having driven them from position to position in a notoriously difficult country, devoid alike of natural and of artificial resources. The numbers of the British, doubtless, were fully adequate to this work. They were greatly superior to the Boers, but not, I think, to a degree much exceeding that which any prudent military man would estimate as absolutely necessary for such a task; considering, that is, the character and extent of the country, the length of the communications, and the general difficulties inherent in all invasions.

I fail, therefore, to see that the ultimate results up to the fall of Pretoria, and during the subsequent disintegration of the Boer forces under continued pressure, are so unsatisfactory as in any way to constitute a reason for that diminution of credit which we call loss of prestige. During the operations which thus terminated, that is, during the process that produced the results, there occurred numerous incidents; some attended by success, some by grave disaster. The latter chiefly require notice, for they are the food for criticism. The advance towards Kimberley was brought sharply to a standstill; the fact being marked by the slaughter at Magersfontein, which we may say ought not to have been. It was not, however, the particular repulse that constituted the check, but the want of numbers, which showed that the advance had been premature. Almost simultaneously came the defeat at Colenso, which postponed the relief of Ladysmith; and upon these two rebuffs followed the strain of national endurance, through the two months of painful uncertainty as to whether the isolated British garrisons could hold out.

Now, I hold no brief to defend the advance on either line at the moment chosen. But I do feel very strongly that it is unreasonable to judge military operations carried on by representative governments on merely military grounds, leaving out of account the absolute necessity of convincing the people represented. The American General Grant certainly did not lack self-dependence or firmness, nor did his subordinate, Sherman, lack eminent military characteristics and acquirements; yet when Sherman remonstrated against the movement round Vicksburg, in 1863, on very sound military grounds of communications, Grant replied that to fall back to a new base for a secure line of communications would so dishearten the nation " that bases of supplies would be of no use ; neither men to hold them nor supplies to be put in them would be furnished." The conclusion was perhaps extreme, but the remark has value. In countries where the voice of the people is mighty it cannot be disregarded, nor can the soldier so separate his military convictions from the popular sentiment as to neglect it wholly. To the utmost possible extent he doubtless should act on strict military reason. Disastrous as the determination appeared to be for a time, I have always applauded White's holding on to Ladysmith, nor have I been able greatly to condemn the risk taken in remaining at Dundee until the necessity of evacuation was not only seen but demonstrated. For the same reason I hesitate to criticise Methuen's advance to the Modder, though it was shown to be premature by the long delay necessary after Magersfontein.

In brief, therefore, while the attempts at advance may have been premature, militarily considered, they were almost unavoidable under the imperfectly understood difficulties of relieving Kimberley and Ladysmith. To hold advanced positions, and to push advance, were inevitable, if only to demonstrate the difficulties and the need of more men ; yet to see the effort of a great empire blocked by two small republics inevitably affected prestige. Failure, until redeemed, cannot but do so ; but, in fact, there was no occasion for disheartenment had the circumstances been intelligently appreciated. I am not aware that in these main operations, up to the standstill in December, there was anything that impeached the general military character of the army. Mistakes in generalship I think there were. These affect the reputation of the general, but they should not that of the nation. Experience is universal that a very large percentage, probably a majority, of able men, men of high promise both in character and acquirement, break down in chief command. The South African war is not in this respect different from others. I know that in our Civil War we had bitter disappointments; and I believe that Dupont, who surrendered somewhat ignominiously at Baylen, in 1808, had stood very high in the esteem of Napoleon himself. Nevertheless, for lack of this correct appreciation, a merely personal defect is carried to the losing balance of national prestige.

There were, however, in both advances incidents of a character which have since too often recurred not to reflect upon the reputation of the army. Passing over questions involving the Commander-in-Chief, as being too essentially personal to warrant general conclusions, the inference prompted by the battle of Colenso, by the deadly surprise at Magersfontein, and by many subsequent episodes, is unquestionably that of inadequacy, or of remissness in subordinate duties, which cannot be reconciled with reasonable requirements of efficiency. Taken singly, any one incident may be due to unexpected causes, or to some one person; but the impression produced — and in speaking of prestige I necessarily deal with impressions — by the numerous surprises, and some surrenders, is that of a proportion of incompetency in the grades of subordinate officers too large to be creditably accounted for. I have even heard surrenders attributed to decay in the fighting quality of the race; than which imputation none can be more injurious to military prestige. This has appeared to me nothing short of absurd, in view of the abundance of good fighting that has been done; and we Americans, as a nation courageous and warlike, but not military, have had experience enough of panic in troops badly officered to dismiss peremptorily any such suggestion. For such discreditable episodes, however, the only one alternative solution is incompetent leadership; and when it is remembered that the leaders in these small affairs are the subordinates, and sometimes the principal subordinates, in large operations, the impression of dangerous unsoundness in the main body is deepened. In contemplating the question of their own acquirements, officers should remember that failure on their part must thus react upon their troops at times, even to the accusation of cowardice. I confess that while I think the prevalent impression of incompetency among officers exaggerated, it does not seem to me unfounded. It errs by neglect to take due account of the mass of good work done; but that is always the case with such criticism, and the loss of prestige which it asserts is not without reason in fact, though immoderate in terms.

If this be so, the defect is precisely one that would be conspicuously felt when the war passed into its second stage, and on both sides took the form of wide dissemination in small bodies, which, however united in some general scheme, were locally self-dependent. This multiplication of small commands necessarily multiplies the chance of inefficiency betraying itself, and not improbably accounts for some mischances. On the other hand, a constant sifting process goes on, and dearly bought experience will remedy this evil. I have no doubt that the efficiency of the force under Lord Kitchener is double now what it was a year ago, both by such process of elimination and by the increase of facility which constant practice bestows even upon those previously well-equipped. There can scarcely be a corresponding gain to the Boers, who already possessed the particular local aptitudes which the British have had to acquire. Of this the makers of prestige have probably taken too little account.

Equally do they fail to take account of the grave difficulties which should qualify the surface impressions produced by the mere prolongation of the trouble. The British Army in South Africa during eighteen months, practically since the fall of Pretoria, has been engaged in a task analogous to that of which the United States Army during the past century has had large experience. Setting aside the savagery in the practices of North American Indians, the Boers have much in common with them, as combatants.   To the adaptation of methods to environment which distinguishes both, as it does natives usually, they have further brought the brain capacity of the white man ; and instead of the tribal tradition of the Indian, they have that of a known common history and of a national existence, which, although excessively loose and unorganized, furnishes a certain bond of cohesion.   Concert of action and persistence are thereby attainable to a degree impossible to the Indians, ever prone to disintegration, and fickle with the fickleness of the savage.   In scope of design and intelligence of direction there is also no comparison.   Let it be added that in both cases the methods of fighting are not external habits, assumed like a change of garments, or superinduced as training upon a recruit, but the outgrowth of surrounding circumstances and everyday life ; an evolution rather than a system, and marked therefore with a spontaneity, a facility, and a readiness, not to be attained offhand by imitators.   As well might a coat be expected to rival the skin in adapting itself to the form and movements of the body.

Forces of this character, acting within their usual environment, and unimpeded by considerations common to men of complex civilization, possess a power of injury and an elusiveness which are enormous; to be matched only by their powerlessness for good, and for self-initiated progress in the civil order. To meet the conditions in South Africa — which, though not unparalleled in kind are perhaps unprecedented in degree, because the brains of white men are utilizing the capacities and immunities of the savage — are needed both adequate methods, probably somewhat original in character, and also familiarity with the particular circumstances which practice alone confers. In this also, and for this reason, Kitchener's command must be much more competent now than it possibly could be a twelvemonth ago.

Some very bad blunders are doubtless chargeable against the management of British detachments in the early and more regular part of the war — blunders against which the training of the officers should have been sufficient prevention; but I cannot see so much discredit, as the apparent loss of prestige would imply, in the mere fact that a final blow has not yet been dealt to the novel and irregular resistance now encountered. The task is one historically and proverbially difficult. I am not an expert in knowledge of our Indian wars; but I have greatly misunderstood what has been said and written, if the most successful methods there applied have not been the joint product of practice and of that species of mental effort which corresponds to invention in industrial life, — a happy thought occurring to an individual whose mind is absorbed in overcoming difficulties with which he has made a thorough experimental acquaintance.[1]   The history of our Indian hostilities is not without its record of grave perplexities, of bafflement, or of occasional appalling disaster; and in the present case, upon a fair balancing of achievement against

[1] To Lord Kitchener, thus pondering, and driven by experiment from one expedient to another, there came the solution of the blockhouse system. The problem before him, and the underlying principle of the plan adopted, have been thus described since the peace. " An army largely immobile," partly from natural characteristics and partly from the absolute necessity of hovering near railway lines, to the protection of which it was tied, "had to cope with one entirely mobile. He used his immobile troops to form artificial frontiers" (the blockhouse lines) "against which the enemy could be driven. It was a heavy task, but he had found the solution, and the Boers were quick to recognize the fact. They saw in the blockhouse line and the drive the end of their struggle, which depended all through upon unlimited power of evasion." — *London Times*, July 12, 1902.

difficulty, I should find ground for increase of hope rather than for diminution of prestige. The man in the street, I fear, judges differently, and his judgment is prestige.

Upon the whole, therefore, while I can see abundant room for criticism of detail, I do not in the military record find cause to warrant loss of prestige. The main defect of the average British officer — that he is not what the French call *instruit*, nor even disposed to become so — has been his trouble historically and always; and it is emphasized now by an enforcement of systematic training in continental armies, and by the United States in their military academy, with which the British authorities are not inclined to comply, either in army or navy. The successes of Great Britain in other times have been attained under this disadvantage. To meet difficulties as they arise, instead of by foresight, to learn by hard experience rather than by reflection or premeditation, are national traits; just as is contempt for constitutions which are made instead of evolved. Personally, if I must choose, I prefer the knowledge given by experience, the acquirements of growth to those of formulated instruction;

but I see no reason why one should exclude the other, to the injury of both. The British officer might possess more knowledge, more reading, more grasp of precedent and principle, without injuring his adaptability. The student's lamp has its part as well as the football field or the cricket ground in equipping an officer.

So much for contemplating the reasonable influence upon military prestige of what has so far occurred and now exists in South African conditions. Upon the broader question of present prestige of the Empire I cannot enlarge, and will limit myself to a brief enumeration of existing factors as they appear to me, with an estimate of the consequent real status of the Empire among the Powers of the world.

First among symptoms is one which, to my mind, gives immeasurable assurance of national power — the sure guarantee of prestige — and that is the progress towards unanimity in the nation, centring round the idea of Imperialism, and finding an immediate impetus in the South African problem. Whatever the faults of a Government, or the failures of an army, a unanimous and sustained national spirit is the vital force, of which prestige is at best but the outward sign and faint reflection. The increase of unanimity throughout the Empire is witnessed both by the movement of the Colonies, and by the rejection of the disintegrating tendency in the Liberal party by its younger and abler members, to whom the future belongs. Imperialism has shown itself an idea capable of quickening national self-consciousness, of bestowing strength of purpose, and of receiving indefinite expansion.

Again, the sea-power of the Empire still stands pre-eminent. I do not here consider the accuracy of the many allegations made, of failure on the part of the Government to maintain necessary progress. Even if these be true, no irreparable harm has yet been done. The Imperial movement of the Colonies, in contributing to the war, is greatly contributive to sea-power. By strengthening the Imperial tie, it gives assurance of local support in many seas — the bases — which sea-power requires; while the military effort, and the experience gained by the colonial troops engaged, render the defence and security of these local bases much more solid than ever before, because dependent upon men experienced in warfare. The foundations are surer.

Again, closely connected with this last consideration is the inevitable superior efficiency of the army at large, Imperial as well as colonial, consequent on this protracted experience of war. I made this remark twenty months ago to an American audience, which I believed to be impressed with the idea of lost prestige, and forgetful of this prolonged warlike practice, obvious as its effect upon efficiency should be. The comment rests now on an even wider and firmer basis than when first uttered. The British army, including colonial contingents, is to-day, to the number of over 200,000 men, a vastly more useful instrument than it could have been two years ago; and this gain will last for at least a decade, as a matter of international calculation, just as the disbanded but tempered forces of the United States remained after the Civil War.

The Confederation of the Empire, whatever shape that may ultimately, if ever, attain, has doubtless been furthered, not hindered, by the war. Community of sentiment and community of action have both been fostered. I would not speak with exaggeration, nor overlook the immense difficulties in maintaining community of interest and of aim between political entities so widely scattered as the component parts of the Empire. The work is one of time, of tact, and labor. I say only that the war has furthered it, and most justly; for from the point of view of the British Islands alone — the Imperial idea apart — the war, so far from being selfish, has been self-sacrificing. It is the Empire, not the Mother Country, that is most interested in this comparatively ex-centric and remote dependency.

In development of power, both local and general, therefore, I believe the war to have strengthened materially the British Empire, and I believe it has likewise given renewed and increased force to the spirit of union, of concentration upon great ideals, without which material strength runs to waste. As an immediate result, I look for the establishment of a group of South African communities, in which the English tradition of law and liberty will henceforth prevail, partly by force of conquest, partly because of its inherent fitness to survive. Of this eminent inherent fitness the

United States of America gives the most signal illustration, because, though so heterogeneous in the composition of its population, the English tongue and the English tradition overbear all competitors, reconcile in themselves all rivalries, and sustain themselves in directive control; modified doubtless, but not weakened, by the variety of foreign influences to which they are subjected.

With these obvious gains — development of Imperial purpose, strengthening of Imperial ties, broadening and confirming the bases of sea-power, increase of military efficiency, demonstrated capacity to send and to sustain 200,000 men on active service, for two years, 6000 miles from home — I do not believe the international prestige of Great Britain has sunk in foreign Cabinets, however it may be reckoned in the streets and cafés of foreign cities. Against this, in order to support a charge of loss of prestige, is set the weary prolongation of the war. Men need not deceive themselves; there is here no even balance. The gain outweighs the loss. I unfeignedly wish that the war, with its sorrows and suspense, might end; but it remains true, sad though the argument is, that the more completely the Boer exhausts himself now, the more convinced and the more final will his submission necessarily be.

I have not thought it incumbent upon me, or even becoming, to enter into discussion of the vexed question concerning the management of the later stage of the war by the Home Government. The conduct of a particular government, like that of a particular general, gives no assured indication of national worth, unless its efficiency or inefficiency proceeds, clearly and inevitably, from causes intrinsically national; as from a close division in national sentiment, or failure in material resources. There is no sign of such division or such failure at the present time; rather the contrary. Whatever the fault or merit of the present Government, challenged as I know it to be by many of its own followers as well as by the Opposition, the point considered in this paper is not the deserts of a group of individuals, but the real power of the nation, on which its prestige should depend. It will be retorted that this begs the question, that the nation cannot put forth its power without the necessary and adequate instrument which a Government is intended to supply, and which, it is urged, this Government does not. The argument, I think, is exaggerated. Governments may do more or less; they may impede or facilitate; but they cannot prevent the exertion of the national will. That they have not done so in this instance is assured — to me — by the very recent assertion, resting on the venerated authority of Lord Roberts, that " Lord Kitchener, in whom we all have implicit confidence, has never made one single demand for men, for horses, or for stores, that has not been immediately complied with." This result is quite compatible with much error, delay, and extravagance; but nevertheless it is the main point secured. The nation does well to be watchful and exacting, for in the wretched plight to which the regular party Opposition is reduced, voluntary organization or individual criticism must supply the corrective of supervision, without which officials never, and private individuals rarely, do their best; but when Lord Roberts can say what he has it is clear that much has been done, even though the most may not have been. Loss of prestige, worth considering, will come when the nation loses heart.

This article, as first penned in November, 1901, ended here. As it opened with comment upon the fundamental primary definition of the word "prestige," let us now, nearly a year later, recur to the secondary accepted meaning, as given by authorities. "Prestige is the moral influence which past successes, as the pledge and promise of future ones, breed." The British war in South Africa, esteemed by many to be of doubtful outcome when I first wrote, has since been carried to a victorious issue. It is now a past success; can it be considered to carry pledge and promise for the future? A correct answer must depend upon due consideration of conditions. A year ago belief in the final result, now realized, rested upon an intellectual appreciation of the decisive facts then attainable, reinforced by a reference to the historical teaching of British warfare in the past. Putting aside the particular merit of individuals, as foreign to the general estimate, success in the present instance, as on former occasions, has been due to national tenacity, and ultimate aptitude to meet conditions as they arise, combined with the essential justice of the national contention. It has been gained despite a certain degree of unreadiness and inadequacy at the outset, which cannot be pronounced wholly excusable. Great Britain has won, as she has before, by national endurance, supported by superior resources, and strengthened by the felt goodness of her cause around which determination could harden. In these substantial strong qualities of national character, the foundations of her prestige are seen to be the same that they were a year ago, and have commonly been in the past. Another demonstration has been added; but her people may hope that she will not further tempt fortune by failing to correct practical deficiencies which have been revealed.

MOTIVES TO IMPERIAL
FEDERATION

MOTIVES TO IMPERIAL FEDERATION

March, 1902.

WITHIN the last twenty years Great Britain has passed through two crises which should appeal strongly to the attention and intelligence — if not also to the practical sympathy — of Americans. Not only have they an analogy to problems we ourselves have met and solved in the course of our national existence, but the result to which they tend, by confirming the power of the British Empire, will probably strengthen likewise the external policy of the United States during the next generation. Interest, due in any case, is emphasized by the fact that the issue at stake has been the same in both these momentous instances. Under all superficial divergences and misleading appearances, the real question about Ireland and about South Africa has been, "Shall Great Britain exist as an Empire,

or shall it fall to pieces by a series of willing
or tolerated secessions?" As Joseph said to
Pharaoh concerning the two visions of the lean
kine and the blasted ears, — the dream is one.
The impetus given to Imperial Federation by
the South African war, the striking root
downward and bearing fruit upward of the
imperial idea, has doubtless been immense;
but the moment really decisive of the Empire's future — as an Empire — is to be
sought in the period when Mr. Parnell's effort
at disruption obtained the support of Mr.
Gladstone. That was the critical instant,
which determined both that the conception
should come to the birth, and that, being born,
it should not be strangled in its cradle.

An impressive article published in 1885, on
the eve of the general election which resulted
in that disastrous stroke of policy, Mr. Gladstone's Irish Bill, both foretold its coming and,
in a spirit of prophecy, perhaps not fully conscious of the scope of its utterance, predicted
likewise the inevitable revulsion of the nation
from a foreign policy marked by constant
feebleness and repeated disgrace, as well as
from an economical propaganda which, what-

ever its possible fitness to a future yet distant, had too far outrun the general sentiment of the people to be practicable. The foreign policy — summed up in the words of Candahar, Majuba, Suakim, Khartoum, and Gordon — was identified by the writer with the name of Mr. Gladstone; the economical programme with that of Mr. Chamberlain. Neither the one nor the other was longer acceptable. The issue indicated, and since fulfilled, was the abatement of interest in internal changes and the concentration of national sentiment upon external policy.

It needed only the announcement of Mr. Gladstone's Irish Bill of 1886 to precipitate the conclusion, for which men's minds were already prepared. The Irish measure, in form a matter of arrangement internal to the United Kingdom, was in essence one of which the gravest bearing was upon external policy; for in principle it involved the dissolution of the Empire. It is to the undying honor and distinction of Mr. Chamberlain that he quickly recognized the issue, and decided without hesitation that the existence of the nation and of the Empire, in undiminished power, involved the interests

of every class of the community, and therefore
utterly exceeded in immediate importance all
projects of social readjustment. Subordinating
to the general welfare the objects with which
he had been most closely associated, he separated himself from the party of his lifelong
allegiance, wherein lay the best hope of accom-
plishing his social programme, and thenceforth
has given pre-eminence to the imperial interests
which he saw threatened. This postponement
of political objects involved a sacrifice of personal ambition, to be appreciated only by recalling the conditions of that time. The same
astute observer, writing but a year later, when
the momentous step had been taken, derided its
finality. " Mr. Chamberlain is the obvious successor of Mr. Gladstone in leadership of the
democracy. It is idle to suppose he would
sacrifice this prospect for the sake of taking
a subordinate position in a Conservative or
even a Coalition Ministry. Sooner or later the
logic of facts must separate him from his present
associates. . . . His assistance to Unionists
is welcome as long as it lasts. Of its essence,
however, it is transitory. Mr. Chamberlain
will return to the Liberal fold, probably at no

remote date." The logic of one great thought, Imperial Unity, the exclusive leading of the single eye, has falsified these predictions; but it is only fair to accept their measurement of what Mr. Chamberlain surrendered by his act.

It is to be apprehended that the recent striking outburst of blended national and imperial sentiments in Great Britain and her colonies, the display of unified enthusiasm sweeping over the various quarters of the Empire, has been an unpleasant surprise to the world at large. In it has been recognized the strong bond of national feeling, oneness of origin and blood, joined to and inspiring the imperial conviction which involves a fundamental unity of policy. If, in the union of the two, deed answered to word, if success followed upon attempt, a power nothing short of new had arisen in the world. The fluttering conception of twenty years ago had become a reality; incipient, perhaps, but with what a possible future! To this, doubtless, has been due in great part the corresponding unanimity of denunciation on the Continent. An unexpected manifestation of power and resolution has elicited an echoing outcry from disappointed anticipation. It is not quite thirty years (1874) since a foreign naval captain remarked to me that in his belief England was a " colosse à pieds d'argile." This impression was general. The phrase voiced a wish as well as a thought; and it may be said that then there was much to justify the implied prophecy, whether it took the shape of a hope or a fear, prompted by dislike or by affection. The tendency of the great money-getting era of trade and material prosperity, of exclusive devotion to purely commercial ideas, of the prevalence of strictly national, internal, domestic interests over colonial sympathies and imperial ambitions, was then culminating to its decline; and one looked in vain for the appearance of higher aspirations and broader views, bearing promise of a fresh spring to national life. A down grade seemed at hand.

After the long supremacy of the dollars-and-cents standards of policy, which arose and flourished in the middle of the nineteenth century, to languish and droop with its closing decades, experience is refreshed, and hope stimulated, by the sight of two great peoples, who speak the same tongue and inherit the same tradition, casting aside considerations of mere monetary cost and abandoning themselves to the domination of a lofty ideal. This the United States did in 1861 under the tremendous impetus exerted by the simple words " The Union," which, cherished almost to idolatry by the boyhood of the North during preceding generations, — as the writer well remembers, — lifted the nation to its feet as one man when disruption threatened. The Union was to us a personification, devotion to which probably afforded the nearest approach to personal loyalty that the spirit of our institutions warrants. Again, although to a less degree, in the Philippines matter, where no such commanding motive or long tradition exists to inspire, there is nevertheless to be found, surely disengaging itself from the confused tumult of impressions inevitable upon decisions taken in the heat of pressing action, the deep conviction, widespread among the people, that here is no mere question of gain or loss, of land or money, but one of moral responsibility. Upon us has devolved, by an inevitable sequence of causes, responsibility to our conscience for an assemblage of peoples in moral

and political childhood; and responsibility
further to the world at large, and to history,
— the supreme earthly judge of men's actions,
— for our course in the emergency thrust upon
us. As such, the United States has accepted
the burden. Its duties are not to be discharged by throwing them overboard, or by
wrapping our political talent in a napkin for
our own national security and ease.

The noble record of Great Britain in Egypt
during the past twenty years, justly considered,
gives inspiration and direction to our purposes
for the Philippines. External conditions are
doubtless most diverse; but, if the informing
spirit be the same, it will adapt itself to the
circumstances, and the good-will find the way
to manifest itself in the damp lowlands and
mountains of the islands as surely as in the
dry Nile Valley. Here the example has been
set us for encouragement; and to cavilers at
the integrity of our purpose, or at the advantage
of our efforts to a subject people, we have but
to cite Egypt, which, like the Philippines, and
but a few years before them, is emerging from
a long period of oppression, to advance through
national childhood to such measure of self-

administration as its people may prove fit for.

As regards the question of federal union, the priority of experience is reversed. However great the difference of conditions here presented to the British Empire and to America, — and it is at least greater than the diversity between the Philippines and Egypt, — the United States has been first to find a solution. The American colonies began their attempt under the difficulty of mutual alienation, due to long standing tradition, and with interests differing probably more radically than those which now exist between the several English-speaking parts of the British Empire. Despite this serious initial obstacle, the thirteen original States, aided later by those afterwards constituted, worked out the problem of union through a prolonged period of perplexity, anxiety, repulsion, and dissension. The final achievement has been so complete that the men of to-day have almost lost the very memory of the antecedent travail, and of the narrow margin by which ruin was more than once escaped. Here, as in Egypt, but with more vital issues, there is the cheering example of success; wrung in this instance out of the jaws of imminent failure. Hence, while the difference of circumstances surrounding the problem of Imperial Federation precludes in great measure any advantage of precedents to be found in the historic path by which the American communities made their way to union, it may safely be argued that, if the informing spirit of desire be present, the adequate motives to a closer imperial bond recognized, the questions of form and method will be solved in the one case as they have been in the other. In both, the purpose and end is the same : to assure unified, or imperial, external action, by the means of an adequate organ, common to all, while preserving the independence of the several parts in their internal affairs. Whatever the particular solution appropriate to either, both present the difficulty of reconciling in practical working two principles, which in terms appear contradictory, whereas in fact they may prove complementary.

Questions of such difficult character do not recommend themselves to practical mankind as political conundrums, in answering which the satisfaction of the intellect is its own sufficient reward. They are not accepted by men

as recreations, but are forced upon them by
urgency. They must supply their own adequate motive, and propose their own reasonable
end, or they receive no attention. Only by
motives most grave, by danger most pressing,
by inconveniences serious in the present and
threatening to be intolerable in the future,
were the American States first driven into a
combination, imperfect and often grudging.
From this, still under the pressure of renewed
urgency, they advanced into a union more perfect in form but still sadly lacking in unity,
either of understanding or sentiment, until,
finally, to avert dismemberment, physical force
itself had to be exerted by those who had come
not only to believe in the Union, but by long
unquestioning devotion to love it supremely.
Mutual jealousy, quite as much as mutual
love, characterized the first efforts of the States
at association. As feeling grew kinder and
warmer, divergence of interest and of political
ideals still tended to preserve and to promote
the element of repulsion, as was shown in the
debates on the acceptance of the present Constitution, and in many incidents of checkered
national life through two generations. Ulti-

mately, translated into broader action, from individual States to groups of States, the last manifestation of the disruptive tendency took on a sectional form, upon a scale so large that the ensuing war was in character rather international than " civil," as it has been commonly styled.

With one exception, there does not exist among the different bodies which should compose a federal Empire of Great Britain the traditional alienation which hampered the movement of the American States in their first efforts towards union. The exception, of course, is Ireland. Practically regarded, it is impossible for a military man, or a statesman with appreciation of military conditions, to look at the map and not perceive that the ambition of Irish separatists, if realized, would be even more threatening to the national life of Great Britain than the secession of the South was to that of the American Union. It would be deadlier, also, to imperial aspirations; for Ireland, by geographical position, lies across and controls the communications of Great Britain with all the outside world, save only that considerable, but far from preponderant, portion which borders the North Sea and the

Baltic. Independent and hostile, it would manacle Great Britain, which at present is, and for years to come must remain, by long odds the most powerful member of the federation, if that take form. The Irish question, therefore, is vitally important, not to Great Britain only, but to the colonies. The considerations that swayed the mind of the Union in the Civil War apply with peculiar force to the connection between Great Britain and Ireland. And let it be distinctly noted that the geographical relation of Ireland to Great Britain imposes as indispensable a political relation which would be fatal to any scheme of federation between the mother country and the remote great colonies. The legislative supremacy of the British parliament, against the assertion of which the American colonists revolted, and which to-day would be found intolerable in exercise in Canada and Australia, cannot be yielded in the case of an island where independent action might very well be attended with fatal consequences to its partner. The instrument for such action, in the shape of an independent parliament, could not safely be trusted even to avowed friends.

The constant lightening of control by the mother country, and the concession of substantial self-government, have removed from the problem before Great Britain and her colonies the initial disadvantage under which the American States drew together; but, on the other hand, the idea of Imperial Federation long awaited the impulse which they received, first from a common extreme danger, and afterwards from their close contact with one another, which emphasized the general injury that mutual independence and inconsiderate action were daily causing. It is not fanciful to say that, as the common dangers to the American colonies from the power of Great Britain, which was to them irresistible unless they combined, supplied the first motive to effectual association; so the needed impulse, urgent if not imperative, was found by the members of the British Empire in the danger and threatened oppression of one of their number by alien blood. The feeling of nationality, the sentiment of one blood and one political tradition, wrought powerfully in support of imperial action in South Africa; and it is a commonplace that action intensifies sentiment.

When the American colonists united in form, however defective, they had made a large practical step towards the sentiment of union, which as a constraining force is even stronger than interest. In that which has been well named "the critical period" of American history, between the War of Independence and the adoption of the Constitution, the love of the Union showed itself forcibly in the utterances even of those who dreaded union on the terms proposed. When we consider the narrow majorities by which these were accepted, it is easy to believe that only the realization in act of the first union, that of the Confederacy, made possible the second,—the federal Union. When the British colonies and the mother country, three years ago, rose together in defence of a threatened brother and child, translating into action an idea nascent but as yet weak in its grasp of men's affections, they also advanced a first stage, the most important stage, in the direction of a further unity, under such ultimate form as their particular relations may demand. The analogy of the two cases is perfectly real. The idea of union was not new to Americans before their Revolution. On the contrary, its advantages were obvious; but all attempts prompted by manifest interest fell abortive, until pressure was supplied by the Stamp Act and its train of incidents. The legislation of the Transvaal, supplemented by the Afrikander Bond, has fulfilled the same office in the history of Imperial Federation; unless, indeed, a prior claim to that honor be established for Mr. Parnell. Not the conception nor yet tentative theories were wanting; but languid inclination had to be quickened into stirring life by contact with pressing occasion.

Two successive dangers, Ireland and South Africa, have thus contributed to the onward movement of imperialism in Great Britain. They have indicated a need and furnished a motive. The first gave birth to aspiration, conscious and definite, towards a higher form of imperial development; corresponding in analogy, though by no means necessarily in outward resemblance, to the "more perfect union" of the once loosely combined American States. The second emphasized the wisdom of such a policy by a concrete example of its advantages. Aspiration, having found its opportunity, was

translated into action; and action in turn rein-
forces and stimulates aspiration by demonstration, and by its powerful effect upon sentiment,
the great motive force of humanity. Happily,
too, for the general impulse, the illustration of
advantage has been afforded in one of the great
colonies, where national self-existence, entire
independence of outside control, and exemption
from the exposure attendant upon an imperial
war, might have a preponderant hold upon
men's minds. The specific utility of the imperial connection to the large secondary members
was shown; for the menace to one of them
came from a State which, though in form internal to the Empire, was in fact and power
external as well as alien.

Similar conditions may well arise elsewhere,
with extreme increase of danger to one of the
great colonies, if severed by independence from
the support of the British navy. Canada,
doubtless, whatever she might lose otherwise,
would find territorial immunity in the policy of
the United States, avowed in the Monroe
Doctrine, — as applicable to her as to South
America; but to South Africa, Australia, and
New Zealand, local difficulties, — such as those

of the Transvaal, and of New Guinea twenty years ago, — would, in the absence of the imperial bond, assume a very different aspect if incurred with a powerful European naval State. These instances also bring into conspicuous evidence the general truth that sea power, the material strength and bond of an Empire the component parts of which are separated by thousands of miles of ocean, is equally essential to the individual security of the several members. Imperial Federation, in action, will manifest itself pre-eminently along ocean and naval lines.

At present the large colonies, while retaining their hold upon the support of the Empire, to the power of which they in turn can contribute much, substantially control all that relates to their internal affairs. Taxation, regulation of commerce, the purse and the sword, are in their own hands. Were they to become immediately independent, no jar would be felt in the continuance of the local administration. The appointment of the governors by the Crown, may, if choice be judicious, materially help to maintain the reality, as it does the form, of political attachment to the mother country; but the actual government is parliamentary, and assumption of independence would not necessarily involve any serious modification of institutions. Further, in two out of the three large aggregations of colonial communities, in Canada and in Australia, there exists now a federal compact, by which bodies but a few years ago politically separate, linked only by common allegiance to Great Britain, are united into one State. British South Africa still remains an assemblage of colonies, with particular local and domestic difficulties of their own, on which it is inopportune here to enlarge.

These are the present political conditions of the principal factors of which an Imperial Federation, if realized, will be composed. It seems inevitable, however, that, when the resistance of the Boers shall have ended, some form of union will be requisite to insure the dominance of British political ideas and traditions throughout the mass of South African colonists; for in such community of sentiment a federal union of the Empire must find the homogeneousness without which it will be but a vain word. The term nation, it is said, applies primarily to community of blood; but I question whether a closer bond is not to be found in inherited acceptance, inborn and inbred, of the same political ideas, fundamental laws, and habits of thought, which regulate the relations and intercourse between man and man, and constitute congeniality. If to these a common tongue be added, environment will have done more to promote unity than it is in the power of mere blood to effect.

It may fairly be questioned whether the phrase Imperial Federation is not something of a misnomer, altogether too broad in its implication. It has obtained currency; and in a general way is understood with as much precision as is perhaps attainable in the present inchoate stage of the idea involved. Are all parts of the present Empire to be admitted as component States in the Federation? Take India as the crucial instance, on account of its extent and population, extremely important elements in state existence; is its constitution, racial, social, and political, such that it could be admitted at the present time as one of several self-governing communities, under the federation of which the affairs of the Federal

State, the interests common to all, and the external policy of the whole, could be administered? Can India be properly described as a State? Without statehood a community can be a member of an Empire, as a dependency, but it can scarcely be a member of a federation.

Logomachies, when nothing more, are unprofitable; but in attempting the solution of such a problem, difficult both on the intellectual and the practical sides, accuracy of expression demands closeness of thought, and is rewarded by increased clearness of vision as to the exact nature of the object desired. I do not propose myself to pursue the interrogatory I have suggested; but apparently the aim of those who desire federation, the importance of which is to me undeniable, should not be so much a federated Empire — is not that a contradiction in terms? — as a federal State, or kingdom, composed of some half-dozen principal members, substantially homogeneous in their principles of government. To this system would remain attached a huge dominion of subordinate communities, differing much between themselves in size and importance, as well as in blood, institutions, and social development, and linked together only by the common rule of the Federal State, as they now are by that of the United Kingdom. The Federal Kingdom and the dependencies, taken together, and in their respective relations of governing and governed, would compose the Empire.

It is such rule and control over peoples not yet fully fitted to go alone that in strictness of phrase constitute Empire. Empire is not a particular form of government. It is a fact, independent of particular methods. The Republic of the United States, already a federal State, has found itself by the impulse and sequence of events in just this position of Empire ; charged with the responsibility of subordinate communities which it would be impossible now to admit to statehood in the federation. Against this condition of empire — actual and inevitable — from which there has been, and is, no escape at once honorable and safe, a small minority of Americans have revolted violently. They regard it as destructive of cherished formulas, political maxims, which are identified with and accurately express the principles of our own national existence and growth, and therefore are assumed,

inconsequently, to apply equally to races entirely different in antecedents and in present
development. Words and phrases, however,
war hopelessly against facts with which they
are inconsistent; nor is there any more curious
instance than this of veritable and futile log-
omachy. To more practical Americans, thus
committed despite themselves to imperialism
after federation, it is impressive to watch a
converse process; to see a consolidated kingdom, a unified State, possessed of an already
existing Empire, feeling its way to perpetuation
and intension of power by means of federation
with those members of its present empire which
are homogeneous to itself.

Imperialism, the extension of national authority over alien communities, is a dominant
note in the world-politics of to-day. Comparatively a newcomer, it already contends for pre-
eminence with commercial ambition, to which
also it ministers. This out-reaching of an
imperialistic arm by all the greater nations,
whether voluntary or compelled by circumstances, constitutes and summarizes the motive
to a closer union than that which now exists
between the members of the British Empire.

In the past, Ireland and the Transvaal have given impulsion; the present and the future have further reason, no less imperious. The conditions have ceased under which independence might conceivably be more advantageous to the larger colonies. If ever true, it is no longer so that the colonial tie brings them no compensative advantage for exposure in war. They are now surrounded by ambitions and confronted by navies which till recently did not exist. Once war meant to them only incidental injury; now it may well mean permanent mutilation to a colony thrown by independence upon its own resources. Not now, if ever, much less now than ever before, can colonial interests be viewed as separate from the politics of Europe and America. In peace as in war, in peace to avert war, or to stay trespass which armed power alone can restrain, each colony now needs the strong arm of the mother country's fleet to sustain its local strength. According to the circumstances, such support may be given either immediately in colonial waters, or by diversion, in Europe or elsewhere, keeping the enemy's battleships remote. In one way or the other it is indispensable. With it the colony will be — not invulnerable, perhaps, but — invincible; without it, immunity can be insured only by the maintenance of a local navy approaching equality with those of Europe.

The greater European powers are now colonially present in several quarters of the globe, and there renew through their colonies the contact and collision of interests which have marked European history. The histories of Australasia and South Africa, possibly of Canada also, are yet to make. Colonial jealousies in turn are transmitted back to the mother countries, and there give rise to diplomatic friction perhaps more dangerous, certainly more frequent, than do questions purely European. In the latter, rulers meet facts of territorial tenure so founded in popular acceptance and mutual jealousies as to give little expectation of facile modification by resort to war. In newer countries, as the history of North America witnesses, the undetermined conditions which exist, and the resultant unrest in men's minds, predispose colonists to jealousies which readily find or give provocation; and strife is promoted by the comparative ease with which great territories may change masters through the fortune of war, as Canada and India, for instance, passed from France to Great Britain in the eighteenth century. In our own day, the political future of the vast tract known as British South Africa is being decided by a war that has found its origin in colonial friction, but to the successful issue of which imperial intervention and sea power were essential. The consequences to Great Britain and her colonies of failure in this case, and the possibilities inherent in the proximity of German East and Southwest Africa, illustrate further the contingencies with which the present and the future of the British Empire will have to deal.

This reliance of the colonies upon the mother nation finds its correlative in the fact that European States in turn rest upon their colonies for maintenance in necessary activities. They can no longer extend freely within their own continent, nor there find adequate markets for their ever increasing production; yet, in order that they may securely expand elsewhere, they must have local support in the several quarters whither their energies reach. This interaction of mother countries and colonies, their reciprocal dependence and importance, are decisive facts, to which development and organization should be given. For local security, or for the assertion of external rights or interests, the colonies cannot as yet dispense with the material force of the home government. Without it they are unequal to a conflict, necessarily in the main naval, with any one of three or four foreign nations whose colonial possessions are near them. A European fleet, on the other hand, must rely upon local bases of action far more than in the days when coal renewal was not a question. For this, isolated fortified stations, like Bermuda and Gibraltar, may be most useful from unique geographical situation ; but in intrinsic value they do not compare with positions which have behind them a loyal continent, with extensive social and commercial organization, such as Canada, Australia, and South Africa afford.

This reciprocal service and utility constitute the chief general and common interest in which the motive to Imperial Federation at present lies. It is not alone, but it is paramount, and will, I think, be found to embrace all the many

minor interests which now, and in peace, tend
to union; for it defends them, and in defending
perpetuates. It is essentially an interest of
general defence imposed by novel and growing
world-conditions. It must be recognized as
covering, not only the local welfare of each and
all the parts, but also the communications between them, chiefly by sea, which may, and in
large measure do, lie remote from any one of
the federation. The several members, and the
highways between them, together make one
whole, to the maintenance of which each even
now contributes. The object of federation is
to promote the security of this imperial system
and its development on firmer lines. To the
general acceptance of this fact of a supreme
common interest must be added on all hands a
hearty disposition to subordinate local interests
to the general welfare, when they clash. Just
here, of course, arises the difficulty of realizing
any federation, especially in its early stages;
later, like everything possessed of inherent
usefulness, federation gains strength by its hold
upon men's affections. The difficulty is very
real, for not only does each member naturally
exaggerate its own claims, but it also tends to

disregard the needs of others, of which it has not immediate experience. Out of touch, out of mind, is the evil genius of all federative efforts, to be expelled only by the superior influence of a dominating affection for the tie of union, through experience of its benefits.

In the order of logical sequence, federation finds its origin and motive force in a common interest, which is the first impulse in the direction of the desired object. The next step is to recognize clearly what is this object, this goal of attainment, by reaching which the admitted interest shall be subserved. The object, I suppose, is to provide the several members with an organism, an instrument common to all, which shall be specifically efficient in the maintenance of the common interests, and inoperative towards strictly individual concerns. This object is loosely styled Imperial Federation, but its particular form and the method of attainment are yet indeterminate. The form of an instrument, and the method of its fabrication, though dictated by the use for which it is designed, are in process distinct from it. The States of the American Union, for example, having recognized certain common interests, formed the common object of making a special provision for the care of those specific interests and of none others. The particular method, — adapted subsequently to the recognition of interest and object, — was a central government fully equipped with executive, legislative, and judicial functions. This form suited them, but most probably may not suit the conditions of the British Empire, the members of which at present seem in the position of having recognized, somewhat imperfectly, a community of interest. Thence has arisen a desire, vague and somewhat feeble, for an object, an instrument, they see not yet just what, to which the common interest may be solely intrusted. When minds are definitely settled on these two points, that they have the interest and need the instrument, thinking men will sooner or later evolve methods. In a recent excursion into that realm of unfulfilled prophecy, the magazines of twenty years ago, I found affirmed the hopelessness of Australian federation. Following by a few numbers, perhaps elicited by this, Sir Henry Parkes stated that all the more thoughtful men in Australia had thought out in one form or another the question of federa-

tion.   The result in Australia is now before us.
Imperial Federation is doubtless a problem
very different in kind, but not necessarily more
hopeless.   The need being recognized, individuals will frame methods, from the discussion
of which feasible measures will result.   Interest
is the foundation of the whole; the object is
the building to be raised thereon, the plan of
which depends upon the needs of those who
shall use it.   The interest, again, is self-
existent; whether men like it or not, there it
is; the object — union in some form — is a
matter of voluntary acceptance and purposeful
effort on the part of those interested.   The
method by which the object is to be attained is
the last in the mental processes.

The contrivance of methods requires close
detailed knowledge of the political conditions
of the several parts, to be attained only by
prolonged personal contact.   A foreigner of
reasonable modesty will here forbear suggestion, but may with less presumption consider some of the obvious circumstances which
make the object more or less desirable, and
the methods of its attainment more or less
intricate.

From the wide dispersion of the principal members it is evident that each one, by acquiescing in any federal bond, enters into such new relations with its fellows as involve a policy external to itself, additional to that already existing towards distinctly foreign nations. Internal affairs remain in the hands of each one; foreign relations continue unaltered; but superimposed upon both come relations to one another on the part of communities geographically far apart, and heretofore practically severed, save for the loose tie now uniting them to the mother country. These relations are new and are external; their maintenance involves an established politic action — policy — distinctly external. Moreover, whatever the nature of the federal bond, there is conceded to it a certain amount of the virtually entire independence previously enjoyed. This will be true of Great Britain as well as of the colonies. At the present writing, in the absence of any federal union, the mother country has entire management of the foreign policy of the Empire. Concern for the interests of the colonies, regard to their possible action in case of serious discontent with particular measures, certainly and necessarily modify the decisions of the British Cabinet. In this way the colonies possess influence; but influence is different from power, less assured in exercise, and less dignified in recognition. Colonial interests, as affected by foreign relations, not only are not in the hands of the colonists, but they have no constitutional voice in determining them. In this chiefly their dependency now consists; and Sir Henry Parkes, whose ideal of Australian independence was not severance from the Empire, but entrance upon a due share in the government of a united Empire, avowed his conviction that there was no possibility of permanent contentment with the status of dependency. Deprecating separate independence, he defined the only alternative to be " sharing on equal terms in all the glory of the Empire." The precision of this phrase is in one respect noteworthy. It does not demand an equal share, but a share " on equal terms." This not only admits, but prescribes, that the power constitutionally exercised by each member shall bear some proportion to the strength contributed by it to the whole. Otherwise there is no equality.

Here, apparently, whatever the method adopted, there will have to be concession on the part of Great Britain. Constitutional restraint upon her present unlimited control of the foreign policy of the Empire, by some clear voting power on the part of the other members, would seem an inevitable concomitant of federation. In return, evidently, the colonies by acquiring a voice in the determination of foreign policy would incur a proportionate obligation to bear the burdens necessary to its enforcement. In place of the purely voluntary and unregulated assistance now given, there must be accepted a compulsory and determinate contribution to the general defence. The amounts may be fixed at the first by an agreement to which all the parties may be voluntary participants; but, unless the federation is to be periodically renewable at choice, — a most unsatisfactory arrangement, — its terms must provide the means for readjustment of obligations, as the several parties advance in strength, at rates probably unequal. This is, in effect, entrusting the power of taxation to a central organ established by the federal Constitution. Unless acceptance of this reap-

portionment of burdens, as provided for by the
terms of federation, is obligatory upon every
member, the federation carries in its constitution the seeds of decay. It is doomed from
its birth; for not only is each member at liberty to withdraw, but the sense of that liberty
will continually sap the sentiment for union
which supplies the spirit of federation, as mutual interest does its body.

We meet here clearly an initial difficulty in
the inequality of population and resources
among the members of the supposed federation. I assume that these would be the United
Kingdom, the Dominion of Canada, the Australian Commonwealth, New Zealand, and the
group of South African colonies, as yet un-
combined. These, at least, would be the principal pillars of the federated Empire. Among
them the United Kingdom is now so greatly
preponderant, upon any ordinary basis of comparison, as to outweigh all the others put
together. As in the case of the province of
Holland among the seven United Netherlands,
this is in effect a cohesive force now, but it
evidently introduces a grave difficulty in the
way of formal federation. Shall the colonies

put themselves under bonds to any central body, in which their total voice is outweighed by the vote of the home country? Could Great Britain accept an arrangement like that of the first American confederacy, where each State, large and small, had one vote? Is there any feasible combination of these two alternatives, such as is to-day presented by the national legislature of the United States?

It is needless to insist upon the practical difficulty as to method. Evidently, to overcome it, motive must be strong. We must fall back upon the common interest which points the way to the common object, leaving to the ingenuity of those directly concerned, or to evolution, — perhaps to both, — the determination of means. The common interest demands increased mutual support throughout the Empire, in view of the new conditions of the world which have transferred the rivalries and the needs of Europe to colonial and other foreign regions. The object is to reach some working arrangement, by which the several contributions of the various parts of the Empire to the general support and defence may be not only determined but enforced. In

peace things may drift along as they are;
but Imperial Federation is needed for probable emergencies, to combine military preparation, to avert war by evident readiness, or
to meet it if it come. It requires, therefore,
the power of the sword and the purse, guaranteed by something more binding than the
voluntary action from time to time of the individual communities composing it. For sustained effort Imperial Federation will be
impotent, unless at the very least the several
members are willing to accept a fixed burden,
periodically determined by some competent
body, external to all, but in the constitution
of which each, of course, has a voice. The
experience of the United States goes farther.
They found it not sufficient to determine in a
lump amount the proportion due from each
member; effective union, efficiency for the
defence of the whole, was not obtained until
power was given to the central government, —
not merely to fix the quotas in men and money
of the several States, — but to lay and to exact
taxes upon the citizens of all the States, passing over the State governments directly to individual men. The power refused by them to

the British Parliament was deliberately, for the sake of union, granted to the Congress of the United States, in which the States and their citizens were severally represented.

This it will be seen was a question of method. Its adoption resulted from long, bitter experience. Only so, and hardly so, was it conceded. It was the final step in the progress to union. Like its predecessors, it was extorted by dire emergency. This imparted the motive; bringing men to desire, as a political object, the organism, the scheme, which out of the States framed the Nation and started it on the road to success. To the American motive geographical nearness contributed much; for the different communities could not help seeing the injury all were receiving from their mutual indifference or antagonism. The members of the British Empire are in this less fortunate. Their remoteness makes less evident the interaction of conditions and events. That the suffering of one member involves injury to each, because of its effect upon the whole, becomes less easy to realize. Motive thereby becomes less clear and less imperative. The impulse to form an object, and to grapple with the difficulties of method which impede its accomplishment, is weakened.

Still, the motives are there. Let each member of the Empire consider, for instance, what it would mean to the general welfare to have an independent and hostile Ireland lying across the access of Great Britain to the outer world. What would the weakening of the chief member of the Empire be to every other? What would a conquered and hostile South Africa have meant to Australia? and beyond Australia, to British influence in the Far East? Can decay of British influence in China be seen with equanimity by Canada, with its Pacific seaboard? For the same reason it cannot be indifferent to Canada whether the British navy and commerce, in war, find their way to the Farther East through the Mediterranean, or be forced to the long Cape route. It is, therefore, matter of interest to her, and to Australia, if a hostile naval power be firmly based on the Persian Gulf. In a way, these are internal questions. They are so immediately, with reference to the Empire at large; but it is easy to see that their determination affects powerfully, possibly even vitally, the

external and foreign relations of the whole and
of each part. One member has just been
saved from destruction by the combined effort
of all, supported by the supreme sea power of
the mother country. This result, too, is internal to the Empire; but is it not also of vast
importance to its external security and foreign
policy? What has made the Transvaal so
formidable to the adjoining colonies and to the
Empire? It is because not only was the population hostile, but the hostility was organized,
armed, and equipped, under the shield of complete self-government. Had Ireland been conceded the substance of Mr. Gladstone's bill, or
should she hereafter attain it, would not her
power of mischief, in case of foreign war,
make such demands upon the presence of the
British navy as seriously to lessen its ability to
protect commercial routes and colonies? She
is to the United Kingdom what the Transvaal
has been to South Africa. The consideration
shows both how important the status of Ireland is to the colonies, and how much, by the
development of their own forces, relieving the
navy of the United Kingdom, they can contribute to its security, and thereby to that of

the commercial routes, which is the common interest of all.

In the question of foreign relations are conspicuously to be seen the advantages of federation, which on the internal side is not without its drawbacks. Its look is distinctively outward, recognizing that there conditions have undergone decisive change. It faces the world, and sees that to do so with success it must show a united body. For that purpose it seeks to find a means, an organ, in which and by which union may be established and maintained. For that purpose it must be willing to endure the internal sacrifices, the inevitable concessions of individual independence, and the burdens of additional expense. For these concessions on either hand there will be compensation. The colonies by entering upon a share in determining the foreign policy of the whole, gain wider scope of action, elevation of idea, increased dignity of existence, and state equality with the United Kingdom, actual in kind, partial in degree; an equality resembling, doubtless, in principle that of the lower house of the United States, where the representation for all the States is the same in character, but in voting power proportioned to the respective populations. Individual colonists would claim and find imperial careers, as the interests and obligations of their native land gained ever increasing expansion in the general growth and interaction of the Empire. To Sir Henry Parkes this seemed, for Australia, a higher destiny than independence; he called it "a rightful share in what may be a more glorious rule than mankind has ever yet seen."

It is not to be denied that superficially, perhaps by force of tradition, the benefit of federation seems chiefly to inure to the mother country. This impression probably derives from the old idea of state property, underlying the colonial relation. Under such a conception, the benefit of the owner of this estate, the mother country, was naturally the primary object in administration. The subordination of the colony was not merely in political connection, but in economical treatment. This was admitted by the American colonists, who, though they rebelled promptly at commercial regulation by tariff, for the raising of imperial revenue, as being indirect taxation, acquiesced in regulation which alleged the benefit of imperial trade as a whole, though they suffered by it.

Such conditions, however, have passed away; and after the temporary domination of the contrary belief, that colonies are of little or no advantage, it is now recognized that in the mutual relation there is reciprocity of benefit, even though there be not equality. Colonies trade more readily with the mother country than with others; and the capital of the latter, other things being equal, seeks investment more readily, with greater feeling of security, in communities kindred in political and legal tradition, and of a common allegiance. The question of military and naval reciprocity of usefulness has been touched on. To this is to be added the wider and grander sphere open to the colonies, as communities and as individuals, when closer relations gain them increasing entry, and opportunity for activity, in the internal administration and foreign policy of a great established State like the United Kingdom. In the present threatening and doubtful question of the future of China are the elements of a world-conflict, in which the British navy is one of the largest among several determinative

factors.   Its strength can be supported and
enlarged by the conditions attendant upon
federation, and the colonies can thus share in
both the benefits and the distinction of influence
upon great political issues; but what of weight
or of prestige can they there display, if severally
independent ?   They may receive the benefit of
the open door, but not the self-contentment of
self-help.   Self-dependence, as distinct from
nominal independence, is to be found in federation, not in separation.   As time passes, it can
hardly fail that the premier and government of
the Australian federation will be greater in
position and wider in activities than the corresponding officials of the several states; and
in like manner a man will be larger in his own
eye and that of the world as a citizen of
Australia, than as belonging to a particular
division of the Commonwealth.   The federation
of the United States exalted irresistibly the
name American far beyond all local designations.   So Imperial Federation will dignify and
enlarge each State and each citizen that enters
its fold.

Imperial Federation proposes a partnership
in which a number of younger and poorer

members are admitted into a long standing wealthy firm. This simile is doubtless not an exhaustive statement; but there can be little doubt that it is sufficiently just to show where the preponderance of benefit will for the time fall. The expenditure of the United Kingdom on the South African war offers a concrete example of this truth, doubly impressive to those who, like the writer, see in this instance great imperial obligation but little material interest, save the greatest of all, — the preservation of the Empire. On the other hand, in view of the spreading collision of interests throughout the world, it is hard to over-value the advantage of healthy, attached, self-governing colonies to a European country of to-day. Blessed is the State that has its quiver full of them. Under such conditions, and with the motives to union that have been presented, it is petty to fasten attention on comparative benefit to the exclusion of mutual benefit. Not by such grudging spirit are great ideas realized, or great ends compassed. Sentiment, imagination, aspiration, the satisfaction of the rational and moral faculties in some object better than bread alone, — all must find a part in a worthy motive; not to the exclusion of reasonable interests, but to their ennoblement by marriage to loftier aims, seeking gratification in wider activities. Like individuals, nations and empires have souls as well as bodies. Great and beneficent achievement ministers to worthier contentment than the filling of the pocket.

Finally, the broadening and strengthening of British power by the progress of Imperial Federation is necessarily an object of profound interest to Americans. In many quarters it will find deep sympathy; in others, perhaps, jealousy may be manifested. For this there is no good cause. The American Commonwealth and the British Empire have had many jars in the past, the memory of which has not wholly disappeared; but more and more clearly are coming into view the permanent conditions that from the first have existed, but until now have been overlaid and buried by the wreckage of past collisions and disputes. In language, law, and political traditions there is fundamental identity; and in blood also, though to some extent differentiated in each by foreign admixture. Coincidently with these, there is a clearly defined and wide belt of geographical separation between their several spheres, — save the one common boundary between Canada and the United States. These constitute permanent factors, tending on the one hand to promote understanding, and on the other to avert misunderstandings. To reinforce these, there is rapidly arising a community of commercial interests and of righteous ideals in the Far East. In proportion to the hold which abiding factors such as these have upon the mind of the statesman, will be the light he finds to thread his way through the passing perplexities of revolving years. The tactical changes of front and redistribution of arrangements, which the incidental progress of events necessitates from time to time, will lack intelligence, coherence, and firmness, unless governed by constant reference to the things which cannot be shaken, and which bear to policy the same relation that the eternal principles of strategy do to the conduct of war.

CONSIDERATIONS GOVERNING
THE DISPOSITION OF NAVIES

CONSIDERATIONS GOVERNING THE DISPOSITION OF NAVIES

May, 1902.

WE have the highest military authority for saying that "War is a business of positions"; a definition which includes necessarily not only the selection of positions to be taken, with the reasonings, or necessities, which dictate the choice, but further also the assignment of proportionate force to the several points occupied. All this is embraced in the easy phrase, "The distribution of the fleet." In these words, therefore, ought to be involved, by necessary implication, an antecedent appreciation of the political, commercial, and military exigencies of the State in the event of possible wars; for the dispositions of peace should bear a close relation to the contingency of war. All three elements form a part of the subject-matter for consideration, for each is an essential factor in national life. Logically separable, in practice the political, commercial, and military needs are so intertwined that their mutual interaction constitutes one problem. The frequent statement that generals in the field have no account to take of political considerations, conveys, along with a partial truth, a most misleading inference. Applied even to military and naval leaders, it errs by lack of qualification ; but for the statesman, under whom the soldier or seaman acts, the political as well as the military conditions must influence, must at times control, and even reverse, decision.

The choice of situations, localities, to be held as bases of operations, is governed by considerations of geographical position, military strength, and natural resources, which endure from age to age; a permanence which justifies the expense of adequate fortification. The distribution of mobile force, military or naval, is subject to greater variation, owing to changes of circumstances. Nevertheless, at any one historical moment, of peace or war, this question also admits of an appropriate fixed determination, general in outline, but not therefore necessarily vague. This conclusion should be the outcome of weighing the possible dangers of the State, and all the various factors — political, commercial, and military — which affect national welfare. The disposition thence adopted should be the one which will best expedite the several readjustments and combinations that may be necessitated by the outbreak of various particular wars, which may happen with this or that possible enemy. Such modification of arrangements can be predicated with reasonable certainty for a measurable period in advance. The decision thus reached may be called the " strategic " solution, because dependent upon ascertainable factors, relatively permanent, of all which it takes account ; and because also it is accepted, consciously and of purpose, as preliminary to the probable great movements of war, present or prospective.

In the particular cases that afterwards arise from time to time, and of which the outbreak of war may itself be one, the unforeseen, the unexpected, begins to come into operation. This is one of the inevitable accompaniments of warfare. The meeting of these new conditions, by suitable changes of plan, is temporary in character, varying possibly from day to day ; but it will generally be found that the more comprehensive has been the previous strategic study, and the more its just forecasts have controlled the primary disposition, — the distribution of force, — the more certainly and readily will this lend itself to the shifting incidents of hostilities. These movements bear to the fundamental general dispositions the relations which tactics have to strategy. In them, on occasions, one or two of the leading considerations which have each had their full weight in the original dispositions, may have to be momentarily subordinated to the more pressing demand of a third. In war, generally and naturally, military exigencies have preponderant weight; but even in war the safety of a great convoy, or of a commercial strategic centre, may at a given instant be of more consequence than a particular military gain. So political conditions may rightly be allowed at times to overweigh military prudence, or to control military activity. This is eminently true, for, after all, war is political action. The old phrase, " The cannon is the last argument of kings," may now be paraphrased, " War is the last argument of diplomacy." Its purpose is to compass political results, where peaceful methods have failed ;

and while undoubtedly, as war, the game should be played in accordance with the well-established principles of the art, yet, as a means to an end, it must consent to momentary modifications, in accepting which a well-balanced mind admits that the means are less than the end, and must be subjected to it.

The question between military and political considerations is therefore one of proportion, varying from time to time as attendant circumstances change. As regards the commercial factor, never before in the history of the world has it been so inextricably commingled with politics. The interdependence of nations for the necessities and luxuries of life have been marvellously increased by the growth of population and the habits of comfort contracted by the peoples of Europe and America through a century of comparative peace, broken only by wars which, though gigantic in scale, have been too short in duration to affect seriously commercial relations. The unmolested course of commerce, reacting upon itself, has contributed also to its own rapid development, a result furthered by the prevalence of a purely economical conception of national greatness during the larger part of the century. This, with the vast increase in rapidity of communication, has multiplied and strengthened the bonds knitting the interests of nations to one another, till the whole now forms an articulated system, not only of prodigious size and activity, but of an excessive sensitiveness, unequalled in former ages. National nerves are exasperated by the delicacy of financial situations, and national resistance to hardship is sapped by generations that have known war only by the battlefield, not in the prolonged endurance of privation and straitness extending through years and reaching every class of the community. The preservation of commercial and financial interests constitutes now a political consideration of the first importance, making for peace and deterring from war; a fact well worthy of observation by those who would exempt maritime commercial intercourse from the operations of naval war, under the illusory plea of protecting private property at sea. Ships and cargoes in transit upon the sea are private property in only one point of view, and that the narrowest. Internationally considered, they are national wealth engaged in reproducing and multiplying itself, to the intensification of the national power, and that by the most effective process; for it relieves the nation from feeding upon itself, and makes the whole outer world contribute to its support. It is therefore a most proper object of attack; more humane, and more conducive to the objects of war, than the slaughter of men. A great check on war would be removed by assuring immunity to a nation's sea-borne trade, the life-blood of its power, the assurer of its credit, the purveyor of its comfort.

This is the more necessary to observe, because, while commerce thus on the one hand deters from war, on the other hand it engenders conflict, fostering ambitions and strifes which tend towards armed collision. Thus it has continuously been from the beginning of sea power. A conspicuous instance was afforded by the Anglo-Dutch wars of the seventeenth century. There were other causes of dissatisfaction between the two nations, but commercial jealousies, rivalry for the opening markets of the newly discovered hemispheres, and for the carrying trade of the world, was the underlying national, as distinguished from the purely governmental motive, which inspired the fierce struggle.   Blood was indeed shed, in profusion ; but it was the suppression of maritime commerce that caused the grass to grow in the streets of Amsterdam, and brought the Dutch Republic to its knees.   This too, it was, that sapped the vital force of Napoleon's Empire, despite the huge tributes exacted by him from the conquered states of Europe, external to his own dominions.   The commerce of our day has brought up children, nourished populations, which now turn upon the mother, crying for bread.   " The place is too strait for us ; give place where we can sell more."   The provision of markets for the production of an ever-increasing number of inhabitants is a leading political problem of the day, the solution of which is sought by methods commercial and methods political, so essentially combative, so offensive and defensive in character, that direct military action would be only a development of them, a direct consequent ; not a breach of continuity in spirit, however it might be in form.   As the interaction of commerce and finance shows a unity in the modern civilized world, so does the struggle for new markets, and for predominance in old, reveal the unsubdued diversity. Here every state is for itself; and in every great state the look for the desired object is outward, just as it was in the days when England and Holland fought over the Spice Islands and the other worlds newly opening before them. Beyond the seas, now as then, are to be found regions scantily populated where can be built up communities with wants to be supplied; while elsewhere are teeming populations who may be led or manipulated to recognize necessities of which they have before been ignorant, and stimulated to provide for them through a higher development of their resources, either by themselves, or, preferably, through the exploitation of foreigners.

We are yet but at the beginning of this marked movement, much as has been done in the way of partition and appropriation within the last twenty years. The regions — chiefly in Africa — which the Powers of Europe have divided by mutual consent, if not to mutual satisfaction, await the gradual process of utilization of their natural resources and consequent increase of inhabitants, the producers and consumers of a commerce yet to be in the distant future. The degree and rate of this development must depend upon the special aptitudes of the self-constituted owners, whose needs meantime are immediate. Their eyes therefore turn necessarily for the moment to quarters where the presence of a population already abundant provides at once, not only numerous buyers and sellers, but the raw material of labor, by which, under suitable direction and with foreign capital, the present production may be multiplied. It is not too much to say that, in order further to promote this commercial action, existing political tenure is being assailed; that the endeavor is to supplant it, as hindering the commercial, or possibly the purely military or political ambitions of the intruder. Commercial enterprise is never so secure, nor so untrammelled, as under its own flag; and when the present owner is obstructive by temperament, as China is, the impulse to overbear its political action by display of force tends to become ungovernable. At all events the fact is notorious; nor can it be seriously doubted that in several other parts of the globe aggression is only deterred by the avowed or understood policy of a powerful opponent, not by the strength of the present possessor. This is the significance of the new Anglo-Japanese agreement, and also of the more venerable Monroe Doctrine of the United States, though that is applicable in another quarter. The parties to either of these policies is interested in the success of the other.

It seems demonstrable, therefore, that as commerce is the engrossing and predominant interest of the world to-day, so, in consequence of its acquired expansion, oversea commerce, over-sea political acquisition, and maritime commercial routes are now the primary objects of external policy among nations. The instrument for the maintenance of policy directed upon these objects is the Navy of the several States; for, whatever influence we attribute to moral ideas, which I have no wish to undervalue, it is certain that, while right rests upon them for its sanction, it depends upon force for adequate assertion against the too numerous, individuals or communities, who either disregard moral sanctions, or reason amiss concerning them.

Further, it is evident that for the moment neither South America nor Africa is an immediate object of far-reaching commercial ambition, to be compassed by political action. Whatever the future may have in store for them, a variety of incidents have relegated them for the time to a position of secondary interest. Attention has centred upon the Pacific generally, and upon the future of China particularly. The present distribution of navies indicates this; for while largely a matter of tradition and routine, nevertheless the assignment of force follows the changes of political circumstances, and undergoes gradual modifications, which reflect the conscious or unconscious sense of the nation that things are different. It is not insignificant that the preponderant French fleet is now in the Mediterranean, whereas it once was in the Atlantic ports; and memories which stretch a generation back can appreciate the fact and the meaning of the diminution of British force on the east and west coasts of America, as also of the increase of Russian battleship force in China seas. Interests have shifted.

Directly connected with these new centres of interest in the Far East, inseparable from them in fact or in policy, are the commercial routes which lead to them. For the commerce and navies of Europe this route is by the Mediterranean and the Suez Canal. This is the line of communication to the objective of interest. The base of all operation, political or military, — so far as the two are separable, — is in the mother countries. These — the base, the objective, and the communications — are the conditions of the problem by which the distribution of naval force is ultimately to be determined. It is to be remarked, however, that while the dominant factor of the three is the line of communication between base and objective, the precise point or section of this upon which control rests, and on which mobile force must be directed, is not necessarily always the same. The distribution of force must have regard to possible changes of dispositions, as the conditions of a war vary.

Every war has two aspects, the defensive and the offensive, to each of which there is a corresponding factor of activity. There is something to gain, the offensive; there is something to lose, the defensive. The ears of men, especially of the uninstructed, are more readily and sympathetically open to the demands of the latter. It appeals to the conservatism which is dominant in the well-to-do, and to the widespread timidity which hesitates to take any risk for the sake of a probable though uncertain gain. The sentiment is entirely respectable in itself, and more than respectable when its power is exercised against breach of the peace for other than the gravest motives — for any mere lucre of gain. But its limitations must be understood. A sound defensive scheme, sustaining the bases of the national force, is the foundation upon which war rests; but who lays a foundation without intending a superstructure? The offensive element in warfare is the superstructure, the end and aim for which the defensive exists, and apart from which it is to all purposes of war worse than useless. When war has been accepted as necessary, success means nothing short of victory; and victory must be sought by offensive measures, and by them only can be insured. "Being in, bear it, that the opposer may be ware of thee." No mere defensive attitude or action avails to such end. Whatever the particular mode of offensive action adopted, whether it be direct military attack, or the national exhaustion of the opponent by cutting off the sources of national well-being, whatsoever method may be chosen, offence, injury, weakening of the foe, to annihilation if need be, must be the guiding purpose of the belligerent. Success will certainly attend him who drives his adversary into the position of the defensive and keeps him there.

Offence therefore dominates, but it does not exclude. The necessity for defence remains obligatory, though subordinate. The two are complementary. It is only in the reversal of *rôles*, by which priority of importance is assigned to the defensive, that ultimate defeat is involved. Nor is this all. Though opposed in idea and separable in method of action, circumstances not infrequently have permitted the union of the two in a single general plan of campaign, which protects at the same time that it attacks. "Fitz James's blade was sword and shield." Of this the system of blockades by the British Navy during the Napoleonic wars was a marked example. Thrust up against the ports of France, and lining her coasts, they covered — shielded — the operations of their own commerce and cruisers in every sea; while at the same time, crossing swords, as it were, with the fleets within, ever on guard, ready to attack, should the enemy give an opening by quitting the shelter of his ports, they frustrated his efforts at a combination of his squadrons by which alone he could hope to reverse conditions. All this was defensive; but the same operation cut the sinews of the enemy's power by depriving him of sea-borne commerce, and promoted the reduction of his colonies. Both these were measures of offence; and both, it may be added, were directed upon the national communications, the sources of national well-being. The means was one, the effect two-fold.

It is evident also that offensive action depends for energy upon the security of the several places whence its resources are drawn. These are appropriately called "bases," for they are the foundations — more exactly, perhaps, the roots — severed from which vigor yields to paralysis. Still more immediately disastrous would be the destruction or capture of the base itself. Therefore, whether it be the home country in general, the centre of the national power, or the narrower localities where are concentrated the materials of warfare in a particular region, the base, by its

need of protection, represents distinctively the
defensive element in any campaign. It must
be secured at all hazards; though, at the same
time, be it clearly said, by recourse to means
which shall least fetter the movements of the
offensive factor — the mobile force, army or
navy. On the other hand, the objective represents with at least equal exclusiveness the
offensive element; there, put it at the least,
preponderance over the enemy, not yet existent, is to be established by force. The mere
effort to get from the base to the objective is
an offensive movement; but the ground inter-
vening between the two is of more complex
character. Here, on the line of communications, offence and defence blend. Here the
belligerent whose precautions secure suitable
permanent positions, the defensive element,
and to them assign proportionate mobile force,
the offensive factor, sufficient by superiority to
overpower his opponent, maintains, by so far
and insomuch, his freedom and power of action
at the distant final objective; for he controls
for his own use the indispensable artery
through which the national life-blood courses
to the distant fleet, and by the same act he

closes it to his enemy. Thus again offence and defence meet, each contributing its due share of effect, unified in method and result by an accurate choice of the field of exertion, of that section of the line of communications where power needs to be mainly exerted.

In purely land warfare the relative strength of the opponents manifests itself in the length of the line of communications each permits itself; the distance, that is, which it ventures to advance from its base towards the enemy. The necessary aim of both is superiority at the point of contact, to be maintained either by actual preponderance of numbers, or else by a combination of inferior numbers with advantageous position. The original strength of each evidently affects the distance that he can thus advance, for the line of communication behind him must be secured by part of his forces, because upon it he depends for almost daily supplies. The weaker therefore can go least distance, and may even be compelled to remain behind the home frontier, — a bare defensive, — yielding the other the moral and material advantage of the offensive. But commonly, in land war, each adversary has his own line of communication, which is behind him with respect to his opponent; each being in a somewhat literal sense opposite, as well as opposed, to the other, and the common objective, to be held by the one or carried by the other, lying between them. The strategic aim of both is to menace, or even to sever permanently, the other's communications; for if they are immediately threatened he must retreat, and if sundered he must surrender. Either result is better obtained by this means than by the resort to fighting, for it saves bloodshed, and therefore economizes power for the purpose of further progress.

Maritime war has its analogy to these conditions, but it ordinarily reproduces them with a modification peculiar to itself. In it the belligerents are not usually on opposite sides of the common objective — though they may be so — but proceed towards it by lines that in general direction are parallel, or convergent, and may even be identical. England and France lie side by side, and have waged many maritime wars; but while there have been exceptions, as Gibraltar and Minorca, or when the command of the Channel was in dispute, the general rule has been that the scene of operations was far distant from both, and that both have approached it by substantially the same route. When the prospective theatre of war is reached, the fleet there depends partly upon secondary local bases of supplies, but ultimately upon the home country, which has continually to renew the local deposits, sending stores forward from time to time over the same paths that the fleets themselves travelled. The security of those sea-roads is therefore essential and the dependence of the fleets upon them for supplies of every kind — pre-eminently of coal — reproduces the land problem of communications in a specialized form. The two have to contest the one line of communications vital to both. It becomes therefore itself an objective, and all the more important because the security of military communications entails in equal measure that of the nation's commerce. In broad generalization, the maritime line of communications is the ocean itself, an open plain, limited by no necessary highways, such as the land has to redeem from the obstacles which encumber it, and largely devoid of the advantages of position that the conformation of ground may afford in a shore battlefield. In so far control depends upon superior numbers only, and the give and take which history records, where disparity has not been great, has gone far to falsify the frequent assertion that the ocean acknowledges but one mistress; but as the sea-road draws near a coast, the armed vessels that assail or protect are facilitated in their task if the shore affords them harbors of refuge and supply. A ship that has to go but fifty miles to reach her field of operation will do in the course of a year the work of several ships that have to go five hundred. Fortified naval depots at suitable points therefore increase numerical force by multiplying it, quite as the possession of strategic points, or the lay of the ground of a battlefield, supply numerical deficiencies.

Hence appears the singular strategic — and, because strategic, commercial — interest of a narrow or landlocked sea, which is multiplied manifold when it forms an essential link in an important maritime route. Many widely divergent tracks may be traced on the ocean's unwrinkled brow; but specifically the one military line of communications between any two points of its surface is that which is decisively the shortest. The measure of force between opponents in such a case depends therefore not only upon superiority at the objective point, but upon control of that particular line of communications; for so only can superiority be maintained. The belligerent who, for any disadvantage of numbers, or from inferiority of strength as contrasted with the combined numbers and position of his opponent, cannot sustain his dominant hold there is already worsted.

To this consideration is due the supreme importance of the Mediterranean in the present conditions of the communications and policies of the world. From the commercial point of view it is much the shortest, and therefore the principal, sea route between Europe and the Farther East. At the present time very nearly one-third of the home trade, the exports and imports, of Great Britain originates in or passes through the Mediterranean; and the single port of Marseilles handles a similar proportion of all the sea-borne commerce of France. From the military standpoint, the same fact of shortness, combined with the number and rivalry of national tenures established throughout its area, constitutes it the most vital and critical link in an interior line between two regions of the gravest international concern. In one of these, in Europe, are situated the bases, the home dominions, of the European Powers concerned, and in the other the present chief objective of external interest to all nations of to-day — that Farther East and western Pacific upon which so many events have conspired recently to fasten the anxious attention of the world.

The Mediterranean therefore becomes necessarily the centre around which must revolve the strategic distribution of European navies. It does not follow, indeed, that the distribution of peace reproduces the dispositions for war; but it must look to them, and rest upon the comprehension of them. The decisive point of action in case of war must be recognized and preparation made accordingly; not only by the establishment of suitable positions, which is the naval strategy of peace, but by a distinct relation settled between the numbers and distribution of vessels needed in war and those maintained in peace. The Mediterranean will

be either the seat of one dominant control,
reaching thence in all directions, owning a single mistress, or it will be the scene of continual
struggle.   Here offence and defence will meet
and blend in their general manifestation of
mobile force and fortified stations.   Elsewhere
the one or the other will have its distinct
sphere of predominance.   The home waters
and their approaches will be the scene of
national defence in the strictest and most
exclusive sense; but it will be defence that
exists for the foundation, upon which reposes
the struggle for, or the control of, the Mediterranean.   The distant East, in whatever spot
there hostilities may rage, will represent, will
be, the offensive sphere; but the determination
of the result, in case of prolongation of war,
will depend upon control of the Mediterranean.
In the degree to which that is insured defence
will find the test of its adequacy, and offence
the measure of its efficiency.

In this combination of the offensive and
defensive factors the Mediterranean presents
an analogy to the military conditions of insular states, such as Great Britain and Japan,
in which the problem of national defence

becomes closely identified with offensive action.
Security, which is simply defence in its com-
pleted result, depends for them upon control
of the sea, which can be assured only by the
offensive action of the national fleet. Its predominance over that of the enemy is sword
and shield. It is a singular advantage to have
the national policy in the matter of military
development and dispositions so far simplified
and unified as it is by this consideration. It
much more than compensates for the double
line of communications open to a continental
state, the two strings to its bow, by its double
frontiers of sea and land; for with the two
frontiers there is double exposure as well as
double utility. They require two-fold protective
action, dissipating the energies of the nation by
dividing them between two distinct objects, to
the injury of both.

An insular state, which alone can be purely
maritime, therefore contemplates war from a
position of antecedent probable superiority
from the two-fold concentration of its policy;
defence and offence being closely identified,
and energy, if exerted judiciously, being fixed
upon the increase of naval force to the clear

subordination of that more narrowly styled
military. The conditions tend to minimize
the division of effort between offensive and
defensive purpose, and, by greater comparative
development of the fleet, to supply a larger
margin of disposable numbers in order to constitute a mobile superiority at a particular
point of the general field. Such a decisive
local superiority at the critical point of action
is the chief end of the military art, alike in
tactics and strategy. Hence it is clear that an
insular state, if attentive to the conditions that
should dictate its policy, is inevitably led to
possess a superiority in that particular kind of
force, the mobility of which enables it most
readily to project its power to the more distant
quarters of the earth, and also to change its
point of application at will with unequalled
rapidity.

The general considerations that have been
advanced concern all the great European nations, in so far as they look outside their own
continent, and to maritime expansion, for the
extension of national influence and power; but
the effect upon the action of each differs necessarily according to their several conditions.

The problem of sea-defence, for instance, relates
primarily to the protection of the national commerce everywhere, and specifically as it draws
near the home ports; serious attack upon the
coast, or upon the ports themselves, being a
secondary consideration, because little likely to
befall a nation able to extend its power far
enough to sea to protect its merchant ships.
From this point of view the position of Germany is embarrassed at once by the fact that
she has, as regards the world at large, but one
coast-line.   To and from this all her sea commerce must go; either passing the English
Channel, flanked for three hundred miles by
France on the one side and England on the
other, or else going north about by the Orkneys,
a most inconvenient circuit, and obtaining but
imperfect shelter from recourse to this deflected
route.   Holland, in her ancient wars with England, when the two were fairly matched in
point of numbers, had dire experience of this
false position, though her navy was little inferior
in numbers to that of her opponent.   This is
another exemplification of the truth that distance is a factor equivalent to a certain number
of ships.   Sea-defence for Germany, in case of

war with France or England, means established naval predominance at least in the North Sea; nor can it be considered complete unless extended through the Channel and as far as Great Britain will have to project hers into the Atlantic. This is Germany's initial disadvantage of position, to be overcome only by adequate superiority of numbers; and it receives little compensation from the security of her Baltic trade, and the facility for closing that sea to her enemies. In fact, Great Britain, whose North Sea trade is but one-fourth of her total, lies to Germany as Ireland does to Great Britain, flanking both routes to the Atlantic; but the great development of the British seacoast, its numerous ports and ample internal communications, strengthen that element of sea-defence which consists in abundant access to harbors of refuge.

For the Baltic Powers, which comprise all the maritime States east of Germany, the commercial drawback of the Orkney route is a little less than for Hamburg and Bremen, in that the exit from the Baltic is nearly equidistant from the north and south extremities of England; nevertheless the excess in distance over the Channel route remains very considerable. The initial naval disadvantage is in no wise diminished. For all the communities east of the Straits of Dover it remains true that in war commerce is paralyzed, and all the resultant consequences of impaired national strength entailed, unless decisive control of the North Sea is established. That effected, there is security for commerce by the northern passage; but this alone is mere defence. Offence, exerted anywhere on the globe, requires a surplusage of force, over that required to hold the North Sea, sufficient to extend and maintain itself west of the British Islands. In case of war with either of the Channel Powers, this means, as between the two opponents, that the eastern belligerent has to guard a long line of communications, and maintain distant positions, against an antagonist resting on a central position, with interior lines, able to strike at choice at either wing of the enemy's extended front. The relation which the English Channel, with its branch the Irish Sea, bears to the North Sea and the Atlantic — that of an interior position — is the same which the Mediterranean bears to the Atlantic and the Indian Sea; nor is it merely fanciful to trace in the passage round the north of Scotland an analogy to that by the Cape of Good Hope. It is a reproduction in miniature. The conditions are similar, the scale different. What the one is to a war whose scene is the north of Europe, the other is to operations by European Powers in Eastern Asia.

To protract such a situation is intolerable to the purse and *morale* of the belligerent who has the disadvantage of position. This of course leads us straight back to the fundamental principles of all naval war, namely, that defence is insured only by offence, and that the one decisive objective of the offensive is the enemy's organized force, his battle-fleet. Therefore, in the event of a war between one of the Channel Powers, and one or more of those to the eastward, the control of the North Sea must be at once decided. For the eastern State it is a matter of obvious immediate necessity, of commercial self-preservation. For the western State the offensive motive is equally imperative; but for Great Britain there is defensive need as well. Her Empire imposes such a development of naval force as makes it economically impracticable to maintain an army as large as those of the Continent. Security against invasion depends therefore upon the fleet. Postponing more distant interests, she must here concentrate an indisputable superiority. It is, however, inconceivable that against any one Power Great Britain should not be able here to exert from the first a preponderance which would effectually cover all her remoter possessions. Only an economical decadence, which would of itself destroy her position among nations, could bring her so to forego the initial advantage she has, in the fact that for her offence and defence meet and are fulfilled in one factor, the command of the sea. History has conclusively demonstrated the inability of a state with even a single continental frontier to compete in naval development with one that is insular, although of smaller population and resources. A coalition of Powers may indeed affect the balance. As a rule, however, a single state against a coalition holds the interior position, the concentrated force; and while calculation should rightly take account of possibilities, it should beware of permitting imagination too free sway in presenting its pictures. Were the eastern

Powers to combine they might prevent Great Britain's use of the North Sea for the safe passage of her merchant shipping; but even so she would but lose commercially the whole of a trade, the greater part of which disappears by the mere fact of war. Invasion is not possible, unless her fleet can be wholly disabled from appearing in that sea. From her geographical position, she still holds her gates open to the outer world, which maintains three-fourths of her commerce in peace.

As Great Britain, however, turns her eyes from the North and Baltic Seas, which in respect to her relations to the world at large may justly be called her rear, she finds conditions confronting her similar to those which position entails upon her eastern neighbors. Here, however, a comparison is to be made. The North Sea is small, its coast-line contracted, the entrance to the Baltic a mere strait. Naval preponderance once established, the lines of transit, especially where they draw near the land, are easily watched. Doubtless, access to the British Islands from the Atlantic, if less confined by geographical surroundings, is constricted by the very necessity of approach-

ing at all; but a preponderant fleet maintained
by Great Britain to the south-west, in the prolongation of the Channel, will not only secure
merchant shipping within its own cruising-
ground, but can extend its support by outlying
cruisers over a great area in every direction.
A fleet thus in local superiority imposes upon
cruisers from the nearest possible enemy —
France — a long circuit to reach the northern
approaches of the islands, where they will
arrive more or less depleted of coal, and in
danger from ships of their own class resting on
the nearer ports of Scotland or Ireland. Superiority in numbers is here again counterbal-
anced by advantage of position. Vessels of
any other country, south or east, are evidently
under still greater drawbacks.

As all the Atlantic routes and Mediterranean
trade converge upon the Channel, this must
be, as it always has been, among the most important stations of the British Navy. In the
general scheme its office is essentially defence.
It protects the economical processes which
sustain national endurance, and thus secures
the foundation on which the vigor of war
rests. But its scope must be sanely conceived.

Imaginative expectation and imaginative alarms must equally be avoided; for both tend to exaggerate the development of defensive dispositions at the expense of offensive power. Entire immunity for commerce must not be anticipated, nor should an occasional severe blow be allowed to force from panic concessions which calm reason rejects. Inconvenience and injury are to be expected, and must be borne in order that the grasp upon the determining points of war may not be relaxed. It will be the natural policy of an enemy to intensify anxiety about the Channel, to retain or divert thither force which were better placed elsewhere. By the size of her navy and by her geographical situation France is the most formidable maritime enemy of Great Britain, and therefore supplies the test to which British dispositions must be brought; but it is probable that in war, as now in peace, France must keep the larger part of her fleet in the Mediterranean. Since the days of Napoleon she has given hostages to fortune in the acquisition of her possessions on the African continent and beyond Suez. Her position in the Mediterranean has become to her not only a matter of national sentiment, which it long has been, but a question of military importance much greater than when Corsica was all she owned there. It is most unlikely that Brest and Cherbourg combined will in our day regain the relative importance of the former alone, a century ago.

In view of this, and barring the case of a coalition, I conceive that the battle-ships of the British Channel Fleet would not need to out-number those of France in the near waters by more than enough to keep actually at sea a force equal to hers. A surplus for reliefs would constitute a reserve for superiority; that is all. The great preponderance required is in the cruisers, who are covered in their operations by the battle-fleet; the mere presence of the latter with an adequate scouting system se-cures them from molestation. Two classes of cruisers are needed, with distinct functions; those which protect commerce by the strong hand and constant movement, and those that keep the battle-fleet informed of the enemy's actions. It is clear that the close watching of hostile ports, an operation strictly tactical, has undergone marked changes of conditions since the old days. The ability to go to sea and steer any course under any conditions of wind, and the possibilities of the torpedo-boat, exaggerated though these probably have been in anticipation, are the two most decisive new factors. To them are to be added the range of coast guns, which keeps scouts at a much greater distance than formerly, and the impossibility now of detecting intentions which once might be inferred from the conditions of masts and sails.

On the other hand the sphere of effectiveness has been immensely increased for the scout by the power to move at will, and latterly by the wireless telegraphy. With high speed and large numbers, it should be possible to sweep the surroundings of any port so thoroughly as to make the chance of undetected escape very small, while the transmission of the essential facts — the enemy's force and the direction taken — is even more certain than detection. A lookout ship to-day will not see an enemy going off south with a fresh fair breeze, which is for herself a head wind to reach her own fleet a hundred miles to the northward. She may not need even to steam to the main body; but, telephoning the news, she will seek to keep the enemy in sight, gathering round her for the same work all of her own class within reach of her electric voice. True, an enemy may double on his track, or otherwise ultimately elude; but the test so imposed on military sagacity and inference is no greater than it formerly was. The data are different; the problem of the same class. Where can he go fruitfully? A raid? Well, a raid, above all a maritime raid, is only a raid; a black eye, if you will, but not a bullet in the heart, nor yet a broken leg. To join another fleet? That is sound, and demands action; but the British battle-fleet having immediate notice, and a fair probability of more information, should not be long behind. There is at all events no perplexity exceeding that with which men of former times dealt successfully. In the same way, and by the same methods, it should be possible to cover an extensive circumference to seaward so effectively that a merchant vessel reaching any point thereof would be substantially secure up to the home port.

The battle-fleet would be the tactical centre upon which both systems of scouts would rest.

To close-watch a port to-day requires vessels swifter than the battle-ships within, and stronger in the aggregate than their cruiser force. The former then cannot overtake to capture, nor outrun to elude; and the latter, which may overtake, cannot drive off their post, nor successfully fight, because inferior in strength. Add to the qualities thus defined sufficient numbers to watch by night the arc of a circle of five miles radius, of which the port is the centre, and you have dispositions extremely effective against an enemy's getting away unperceived. The vessels nearest in are individually so small that the loss of one by torpedo is militarily immaterial; moreover, the chances will by no means all be with the torpedo-boat. The battle-fleet, a hundred or two miles distant it may be, and in a different position every night, is as safe from torpedo attack as ingenuity can place it. Between it and the inside scouts are the armored cruisers, faster than the hostile battle-fleet, stronger than the hostile cruisers. These are tactical dispositions fit for to-day; and in essence they reproduce those of St. Vincent before Brest, and his placing of

Nelson at Cadiz with an inshore squadron, a century ago. "A squadron of frigates and cutters plying day and night in the opening of the Goulet; five ships-of-the-line anchored about ten miles outside; and outside of them again three of-the-line under sail." The main body, the battle-fleet of that time, was from twenty-five to forty miles distant, — the equivalent in time of not less than a hundred miles to-day.

Keeping in consideration these same waters, the office and function of the Channel Fleet may be better realized by regarding the battle-ships as the centre, from which depart the dispositions for watching, not only the enemy's port, but also the huge area to seaward which it is desired to patrol efficiently for the security of the national commerce. Take a radius of two hundred miles; to it corresponds a semi-circle of six hundred, all within Marconi range of the centre. The battle-fleet never separates. On the far circumference move the lighter and swifter cruisers; those least able to resist, if surprised by an enemy, but also the best able to escape, and the loss of one of which is inconsiderable, as of the inner cruisers off the port. Between them and the fleet are the heavier cruisers, somewhat dispersed, in very open order, but in mutual touch, with a squadron organization and a plan of concentration, if by mischance an enemy's division come upon one of them unawares. Let us suppose, under such a danger, they are one hundred miles from the central body. It moves out at twelve miles an hour, they in at fifteen. Within four hours the force is united, save the light cruisers. These, as in all ages, must in large measure look out for themselves, and can do so very well.

Granting, as required by the hypothesis, equality in battle-ships and a large preponderance in cruisers, — not an unreasonable demand upon an insular state, — it seems to me that for an essentially defensive function there is here a fairly reliable, systematized, working disposition. It provides a semi-circumference of six hundred miles, upon reaching any point of which a merchant ship is secure for the rest of her homeward journey. While maintained, the national frontier is by so much advanced, and the area of greatest exposure for the merchant fleet equally reduced. Outside this, cruising as formerly practised can extend very far a protection, which, if less in degree, is still considerable. For this purpose, in my own judgment, and I think by the verdict of history, dissociated single ships are less efficient than cruiser-squadrons, such as were illustrated by the deeds of Jean Bart and Pellew. One such, a half-dozen strong, west of Finisterre, and another west of Scotland, each under a competent chief authorized to move at discretion over a fairly wide area, beyond the bailiwick of the commander-in-chief, would keep enemies at a respectful distance from much more ground than he actually occupies; for it is to be remembered that the opponent's imagination of danger is as fruitful as one's own.

In conception, this scheme is purely defensive. Incidentally, if opportunity offer to injure the enemy it will of course be embraced, but the controlling object is to remove the danger to home commerce by neutralizing the enemy's fleet. To this end numbers and force are calculated. This done, the next step is to consider the Mediterranean from the obvious and inevitable military point of view that it is the one and only central position, the assured control of which gives an interior line of operations from the western coast of Europe to the eastern waters of Asia. To have assured safety to the home seas and seaboard is little, except as a means to further action; for, if to build without a foundation is disastrous, to lay foundations and not to be able to build is impotent, and that is the case where disproportioned care is given to mere defensive arrangements. The power secured and stored at home must be continually transmitted to the distant scene of operations, here assumed, on account of the known conditions of world politics, to be the western Pacific, which, under varying local designations, washes the shores of the Farther East.

It has been said that in the Mediterranean, as the principal link in the long chain of communications, defence and offence blend. Moreover, since control here means assured quickest transmission of reinforcements and supplies in either direction, it follows that, while preponderance in battle-ship force is essential in the Far East, where if war occurs the operations will be offensive, such predominance in the Mediterranean, equally essential in kind, must be much greater in degree. In

fact, the offensive fleet in the Eastern Seas and
the defensive fleet in the Channel are the two
wings, or flanks, of a long front of operations,
the due security of both of which depends upon
the assured tenure of the central position.
Naturally, therefore, the Mediterranean fleet,
having to support both, possibly even to detach hurriedly to one or the other, has in itself that combination of defensive and offensive character which ordinarily inheres in sea
communications as such.

If this assertion be accepted in general statement, it will be fortified by a brief consideration of permanent conditions; with which it
is further essential to associate as present temporary factors the existing alliances between
France and Russia, Great Britain and Japan.
The Triple Alliance, of the renewal of which
we are assured, does not contemplate among
its objects any one that is directly affected by
the control of the Mediterranean. Should an
individual member engage in war having its
scene there, it would be as a power untrammelled by this previous engagement.

History and physical conformation have
constituted unique strategic conditions in the

Mediterranean. To history is due the existing tenure of positions, the bases, of varying
intrinsic value, and held with varying degrees
of power and firmness by several nations in
several quarters. To examine these minutely
and weigh their respective values as an element of strategic effect would be indeed essential to the particular planning of a naval campaign, or to the proper determination of the
distribution of naval force, with a view to the
combinations open to one's self or the enemy;
but a paper dealing with general conditions
may leave such detailed considerations to those
immediately concerned. It must be sufficient
to note the eminently central position of Malta,
the unique position of Gibraltar, and the ex-
centric situation of Toulon relatively to the
great trade route. By conformation the Mediterranean has, besides the artificial canal, —
the frailest and most doubtful part of the chain,
— at least three straits of the utmost decisive
importance, because there is to them no alternative passage by which vessels can leave the
sea, or move from one part of it to another.
In the Caribbean Sea, which is a kind of Mediterranean, the multiplicity of islands and pas-

sages reduces many of them to inconsequence, and qualifies markedly the effect of even the most important; but, in the Mediterranean, the Dardanelles, Gibraltar, and the belt of water separating the toe of Italy from Cape Bon in Africa, constitute three points of transit which cannot be evaded. It is true that in the last the situation of the island of Sicily allows vessels to go on its either side; but the surrounding conditions are such that it is scarcely possible for a fleet to pass undetected by an adversary making due use of his scouts. These physical peculiarities, conjointly with the positions specified, are the permanent features, which must underlie and control all strategic plans of Mediterranean Powers, among whom Russia must be inferentially included.

Geographically, Great Britain is an intruder in the Mediterranean. Her presence there at all, in territorial tenure, is distinctively military. This is witnessed also by the character of her particular possessions. Nowhere does the vital energy of sea power appear more conspicuously, as self-expansive and self-dependent. To its historical manifestation is due the acquisitions which make the strength of her present position; but, as in history, so now, sea power itself must continue to sustain that which it begat. The habitual distribution of the warships of the United Kingdom must provide for a decisive predominance here, upon occasion arising, over any probable combination of enemies. Such provision has to take account not only of the total force of hostile divisions within and without the Mediterranean, but of movements intended to transfer one or more from or to that sea from other scenes of operations. Prevention of these attempts is a question, not of numbers chiefly, but of position, of stations assigned, of distribution. Predominance, to be militarily effectual, means not only an aggregate superiority to the enemy united, but ability to frustrate, before accomplishment, concentrations which might give him a local superiority anywhere. This is a question of positions more even than of numbers. In the Mediterranean, as the great centre, these two factors must receive such mutual adjustment as shall outweigh the combination of them on the part of the adversary. Where one is defective the other must be increased. The need is the more emphatic when

the nation itself is external and distant from
the sea, while possible antagonists, as Russia
and France, are territorially contiguous; for
it can scarcely be expected that the Russian
Black Sea fleet would not force its way through
the Dardanelles upon urgent occasion.

Evidently, too, Japan cannot in the near
future contribute directly to maintain Great
Britain in the Mediterranean. On the contrary, the declarations of Russia and France
make plain that, if war arise, Japan must be
supported in the Far East by her ally against
a coalition, the uncertain element of which is
the force that France will feel able to spare
from her scattered, exposed interests. Russia
labors under no such distraction; her single-
ness of eye is shown by the fact that the more
efficient, and by far the larger part, of her so-
called Baltic fleet is now in the waters of China.
In numbers and force she has there a substantial naval equality with Japan, but under
a disadvantage of position like that of Great
Britain in the Mediterranean, in being remote
from the centre of her power, imperfectly based,
as yet, upon local resources, and with home
communications by the shortest route gravely

uncertain. Under these circumstances the decided step she has taken in the reinforcement of her Eastern Navy, carries the political inference that she for the present means to seek her desired access to unfrozen waters in Eastern Asia, preferably to the Mediterranean or the Persian Gulf. Having in view local difficulties and antagonistic interests elsewhere, this conclusion was probably inevitable; but its evident acceptance is notable.

For Great Britain it is also most opportune; and this raises a further question, attractive to speculative minds, viz.: whether the Anglo-Japanese agreement has had upon Russia a stimulating or a deterrent effect? If it has increased her determination to utilize her present advantages, as represented in Port Arthur and its railroad, it would be in the direct line of a sound British policy; for it fixes the reasonable satisfaction of Russia's indisputable needs in a region remote from the greater interests of Great Britain, yet where attempts at undue predominance will elicit the active resistance of many competitors, intent upon their own equally indisputable rights. The gathering of the eagles on the coasts of China is manifest to the dullest eye.   But should the alliance have the contrary effect of checking Russian development in that direction, her irrepressible tendency to the sea is necessarily thrown upon a quarter — the Levant or Persia — more distinctly ominous, and where, in the last named at least, Great Britain would find no natural supporter, enlisted by similarity of interest.   The concentration of Russian ships in the East, taken in connection with the general trend of events there, is, however, as clear an indication of policy as can well be given.

In connection with the substantial numerical equality of Japan and Russia is to be taken, as one of the ascertained existing conditions, instituted so recently as to have a possible political significance, the reorganization of the French divisions beyond Suez into a single command, and the numbers thereto assigned.   It is not to be supposed that this new disposition has been adopted without consideration of the new combinations indicated by the Anglo-Japanese treaty.   It may even be in direct consequence.   The relative strengths of this extensive eastern command and of the French Mediterranean fleet should in close measure reflect the official consciousness of the general naval situation, and of the power of France to give support to her recognized ally; directly in the East, and indirectly by military influence exerted upon the Mediterranean. Supposing Great Britain, on the other hand, to have made provision for the defensive control of the approaches to her home ports, how will she, and how can she, assure the joint ascendency of herself and her ally in the Farther East, the scene of the offensive, and her own single preponderance in the Mediterranean, the main link in the communications? These are the two intricate factors for consideration, calling for plans and movements not primarily defensive but offensive in scope. For France and for Great Britain, as a party to an alliance, the question is urgent, " How far can I go, how much spare from the Mediterranean to the East? In assisting my ally there, unless I bring him predominance, or at least nearly an equality, I waste my substance, little helping him. If paralyzed in the Mediterranean, thrown on a mere defensive, my force in the East is practically cut off. Like a besieged garrison, it may endure till relieved; but the situation is critical while it lasts, and carries imminent possibilities of disaster."

In approaching a military subject of this character it is necessary first and for all to disabuse the mind of the idea that a scheme can be devised, a disposition imagined, by which all risk is eliminated. Such an attractive condition of absolute security, if realized, would eliminate all war along with its risks. A British distribution, most proper for the Mediterranean alone, may entail the danger that a hostile body may escape into the Atlantic, may unite with the Brest and Cherbourg divisions against the Channel Fleet, and overwhelm the latter. True; but imagination must work both ways. It may also be that the escape cannot but be known at Gibraltar, telegraphed to England, and the fleet warned betimes so that the reserve ships, which give it a superiority to either detachment of the enemy, might join, and that its scouts, stationed as previously suggested, would gain for it the two hours of time needed to deal decisively with one division before the other turns up. These probabilities, known to the enemy, affect his actions just as one's own risks move one's self. Listen to Nel-

son contemplating just this contingency. " If
the Ferrol squadron joins the Toulon, they will
much outnumber us, but in that case I shall
never lose sight of them, and Pellew " (from
before Ferrol) " will soon be after them." But
he adds, confirmatory of the need of numerous
scouts, then as now, " I at this moment want
ten frigates or sloops, when I believe neither
the Ferrol or Toulon squadron could escape
me." By this, I understand, is clearly inti-
mated that he could look out both ways, in-
tercept the first comer, frustrate the junction,
and beat them in detail. If not before the
action, Pellew would arrive in time to repair
Nelson's losses and restore equality. The
change in modern conditions would favor the
modern Pellew more than the adversary.

So again disturbing political possibilities
must be reasonably viewed. It may be that
the whole Continent not only dislikes Great
Britain, but would willingly combine for her
military destruction; and that, if war begin,
such a combination may come to pass. It may
be; but this at least is certain, that interest,
not liking, will decide so grave a matter.
In the calculation of final issues, of national

expenditure, of profit and loss, of relative national predominance resulting from a supposed success, I incline to think that Imperial Federation will be a far less difficult achievement than framing such a coalition. If the two dual alliances, the mutual opposition of which is apparent, come to blows, Germany may see it to her interest to strike hands with Russia and France; but it seems to me it would be so much more her interest to let them exhaust themselves, to the relief of her two flanks, that I find it difficult to believe she would not herself so view the question. There is one qualifying consideration. Germany cannot but wish a modification in the effect exerted upon her maritime routes by the position of Great Britain, already noted. As geographical situation cannot be changed, the only modification possible is the decrease of Great Britain's power by the lessening of her fleet. But, grant that object gained by such coalition, what remains? A Channel dominated by the French Navy no longer checked by the British; whereas with the latter as an ally the Channel would be almost as safe as the Kiel canal. If this remark is sound, it is but an illustration of the choice of difficulties presented by attempts to change permanent conditions by artificial combinations. As a matter of fact, no single power in Europe, save possibly Russia, is individually so weighty as to see without apprehension the effective elimination of any one factor in the present balance of power. The combined position and numbers of Russia do give her a great defensive security in her present tenures.

Admitting the Mediterranean to be distinctively and pre-eminently the crucial feature in any strategic scheme that contemplates Europe and the Farther East as the chief factors of interest, the positions before enumerated, in conjunction with the relative forces of the fleets, constitute the initial strategic situation. Assuming, as is very possible, that the decisive predominance, local or general, desired by either party, does not yet exist, the attempt of each must be to reach some preponderance by playing the game of war; by such applied pressure or strategic movements as shall procure a decisive momentary preponderance in some quarter, the due use of which, by the injury done the enemy, shall establish a permanent and decisive superiority. This is the one object of war scientifically — or better, artistically — considered. The nation that begins with the stronger fleet should initiate some offensive action, with the object of compelling the enemy to fight. This the latter cannot do, unless already in adequate strength at some one point, except by undertaking to combine his divided forces so as to effect a concentration in some quarter. The movements necessary to accomplish this are the opportunity of the offensive, to strike the converging divisions before their junction gives the desired local superiority. Herein is the skill; herein also the chance, the unexpected, the risk, which the best authorities tell us are inseparable from war, and constitute much of its opportunity as of its danger.

How shall the superior fleet exercise the needed compulsion? Ships cannot invade territory, unless there be unprotected navigable rivers. The stronger navy therefore cannot carry war beyond the sea-coast, home to the heart of the enemy, unless indeed its nation in addition to controlling the sea, can transport an overpowering force of troops. Of this the Transvaal war offers an illustration. Possibly, a disabling blow to the British fleet by the navy of one of the great continental armies might present a somewhat similar instance; but when the British fleet is thus enfeebled, Great Britain will be exposed to the conditions which it must be her own first effort, with her supreme navy, to impose on an opponent. Under such circumstances, there will be no need for an enemy to land an invading host on British soil. The interception of commerce at a half-dozen of the principal ports will do the work as surely, if less directly. Similarly, while the British Navy is what it is, the destruction of an enemy's commerce, not only by scattered cruisers at sea, but by a systematized, coherent effort directed against his ports and coasts, both home and colonial, must be the means of inflicting such distress and loss as shall compel his fleet to fight; or, if it still refuse, shall sap endurance by suffering and extenuation.

To effect this requires a battle-fleet superior in the aggregate to the one immediately opposed to it by at least so many ships as shall suffice to allow a constant system of reliefs. The battle-fleet is the solid nucleus of power. From it radiates the system of cruisers by which the trade blockade is maintained in technical, and as far as may be, in actual, efficiency. In case of hostilities with France, for example, the blockade of a principal commercial port, like Havre or Marseille, may be sustained in local efficiency by cruisers; but the security of these, and consequently the maintenance of the blockade, will depend upon such proximity of the battle-fleet as will prevent the French divisions at Cherbourg, Brest, or Toulon, from attacking them, except at great risk of being compelled to an engagement which it is presumably the specific aim of the British fleet to force. " Not blockade but battle is my aim," said Nelson: " on the sea alone we hope to realize the hopes and expectations of our country." A successful battle in any one quarter clears up the whole situation; that is, in proportion to the results obtained. This qualification is always to be borne in mind by a victorious admiral; for the general relief to his nation will correspond to the use made by him of the particular advantage gained. More or fewer of his ships will be liberated from their previous tasks, and can reinforce the station where the most assured predominance is desired. This by our analysis is the Mediterranean.

History has more than once shown how severe a compulsion may be exerted over an extensive coast by proper dispositions. Where a formidable, though inferior, navy lies in the ports of the blockaded state, the position and management of the battle-fleet, on either side, is the critical military problem. The task of the cruisers is simple, if arduous; to keep near the port assigned them, to hold their ground against equals, to escape capture by superior force. The battle-fleet must be so placed as effectually to cover the cruisers from the enemy's fleet, without unduly exposing itself; above all to torpedo attack. It must be on hand, not only to fight, but to chase to advantage, to make strategic movements, perhaps extensive in range, at short notice. War is a business of positions. Its position, suitably chosen, by supporting the cruiser force, covers the approaches of the national commerce, and also maintains both the commercial blockade and the close watch of the military ports. It may be noted that the commercial blockade is offensive in design, to injure the enemy and compel him to fight, while the other specified functions of the vessels are defensive. We therefore have here again a combination of the two purposes in a single disposition.

For some time to come nations distinctively European must depend upon the Mediterranean as their principal military route to the Far East. In the present condition of the Siberian railroad, Russia shares this common lot. While the other States have no land route whatever, hers is still so imperfect as not to constitute a valid substitute. Moreover, whatever resources of moderate bulk may be locally accumulated, — coal, provisions, ammunition, and stores of various kinds, — reinforcements of vessels, or reliefs to ships disabled by service or in battle can go only by sea. Guns beyond a certain calibre are in like case. Every consideration emphasizes the importance of the Mediterranean. To it the Red Sea is simply an annex, the military status of which will be determined by that of its greater neighbor, qualified in some measure by the tenure of Egypt and Aden.

On the farther side of the isthmus the naval operations throughout Eastern seas will depend for sustained vigor upon contact militarily maintained with the Mediterranean, and through that with home. In these days of cables, the decisive importance of Malta to India, recognized by Nelson and his contemporaries, is affirmed with quadruple force of the sea in which Malta is perhaps the most conspicuously important naval position. Reinforcements sent by the Cape, whether west or east, can always be anticipated at either end of the road by the Power which holds the interior line.

As regards special dispositions for the Eastern seas, embracing under that name all from Suez to Japan, the same factors — numbers and position — dictate distribution. To a central position, if such there be, must be assigned numbers adequate to immediate superiority, in order to control commercial routes, and to operate against the enemy whose approximate force and position are known. Such assignment keeps in view, necessarily, the possibilities of receiving reinforcements from the Mediterranean, or having to send them to China. Ceylon, for example, if otherwise suitable, is nearly midway between Suez and Hong-Kong; in round numbers, 3000 miles from each. Such a position favors a force of battle-ships as an advanced squadron from the Mediterranean, and would be a provision against a mishap at the canal interrupting reinforcements eastward. Position, with its two functions of distance and resources; there is nothing more prominent than these in Napoleon's analysis of a military situation. Numbers go, as it were, without saying. Where the power was his he multiplied them; but he always remembered that position multiplies spontaneously. He who has but half-way to go does double work. This is the privilege of central position.

The question of the Eastern seas introduces naturally the consideration of what the great self-governing colonies can do, not only for their own immediate security, and that of their trade, but for the general fabric of Imperial naval action, in the coherence of which they will find far greater assurance than in merely local effort. The prime naval considerations for them are that the British Channel Fleet should adequately protect the commerce and shores of the British Islands, and that the Mediterranean Fleet should insure uninterrupted transit for trade and for reinforcements. These effected and maintained, there will be no danger to their territory; and little to their trade except from single cruisers, which will have a precarious subsistence as compared with their own, based upon large self-support-ing political communities. Australasia, how-ever, can undoubtedly supply a very important factor, that will go far to fortify the whole British position in the Far East. A continent in itself, with a thriving population, and willing, apparently, to contribute to the general naval welfare, let it frame its schemes and base its estimates on sound lines, both naval and im-perial; naval, by allowing due weight to battle force; imperial, by contemplating the whole, and recognizing that local safety is not always best found in local precaution. There is a military sense, in which it is true that he who loses his life shall save it.

In the Eastern seas, Australia and China mark the extremities of two long lines, the junction of which is near India; let us say, for sake of specificness, Ceylon. They are off-shoots, each, of one branch, the root of which under present conditions, is the English Chan-nel, and the trunk the Mediterranean. Now it is the nature of extremities to be exposed. To this our feet, hands, and ears bear witness, as does the military aphorism about salients; but while local protection has its value in these several cases, the general vigor and sustenance of the organism as a whole is the truer dependence. To apply this simile: it appears to me that the waters from Suez eastward should be regarded as a military whole, vitally connected with the system to the westward, but liable to temporary interruption at the Canal, against which precaution must be had. This recognizes at once the usual dependence upon the Channel and the Mediterranean, and the coincident necessity of providing for independent existence on emergency. In the nature of things there must be a big detachment east of Suez; the chance of its being momentarily cut off there is not so bad as its being stalled on the other side, dependent on the Cape route to reach the scene. But for the same reason that the Mediterranean and Malta are strategically eminent, because central, (as is likewise the Channel with reference to the North Sea and Atlantic), the permanent strategic centre of the Eastern seas is not by position in China, nor yet in Australia. It is to be found rather at a point which, approximately equidistant from both, is also equidistant from the Mediterranean and the East. Permanent, I say; not as ignoring that the force which there finds its centre may have to remove, and long to remain, at one extremity or another of the many radii thence issuing, but because there it is best placed to move in the shortest time in any one of the several directions. That from the same centre it best protects the general commercial interests is evident from an examination of the maps and of commercial returns.

Whether the essential unity of scope in naval action east of Suez should receive recognition by embracing Australia, China, and India, under one general command, with local subordinates, is a question administrative as well as strategic. As military policy it has a good side; for commanders previously independent do not always accept ungrudgingly the intrusion of a superior because of emergency of war. Military sensitiveness cannot prudently be left out of calculations. There would be benefit also in emphasizing in public consciousness the essential unity of military considerations, which

should dominate the dispositions of the fleet.
Non-professional — and even military — minds
need the habit of regarding local and general
interests in their true relations and proportions.
Unless such correct appreciation exist, it is
hard to silence the clamor for a simple local
security, which is apparent but not real, because
founded on a subdivision and dissemination of
force essentially contrary to sound military
principle. What Australasia needs is not her
petty fraction of the Imperial navy, a squadron
assigned to her in perpetual presence, but an
organization of naval force which constitutes a
firm grasp of the universal naval situation.
Thus danger is kept remote; but, if it should
approach, there is insured within reaching distance an adequate force to repel it betimes.
There may, however, be fairly demanded the
guarantee for the fleet's action, in a development of local dock-yard facilities and other
resources which shall insure its maintenance in
full efficiency if it have to come.

In this essential principle other colonies
should acquiesce. The essence of the matter
is that local security does not necessarily, nor
usually, depend upon the constant local presence

of a protector, ship or squadron, but upon general dispositions. As was said to and of Rodney, " Unless men take the great line, as you do, and consider the King's whole dominions as under their care, the enemy must find us unprepared somewhere. It is impossible to have a superior fleet in every part."

It is impossible; and it is unnecessary, granting the aggregate superiority at which Great Britain now aims. In the question of the disposition of force three principal elements are distinguishable in the permanent factors which we classify under the general head of " position." These are, the recognition of central positions, of interior lines — which means, briefly, shorter lines — and provision of abundant local dock-yard equipment in its widest sense. These furnish the broad outline, the skeleton of the arrangement. They constitute, so to say, the qualitative result of the analysis which underlies the whole calculation. Add to it the quantitative estimate of the interests at stake, the dangers at hand, the advantages of position, in the several quarters, and you reach the assignment of numbers, which shall make the dry bones live with all the energy of flesh and blood in a healthy body ; where each member is supported, not by a local congestion of vitality, but by the vigor of the central organs which circulate nourishment to each in proportion to its needs.

THE PERSIAN GULF AND
INTERNATIONAL RELATIONS

THE PERSIAN GULF AND INTERNATIONAL RELATIONS

June, 1902.

THE American whom above all others his countrymen delight to honor, more even to-day than a century ago, as his sober wisdom and unselfish patriotism stand in stronger relief on the clear horizon of the past, when he took leave of public life, cautioned his fellow-citizens of that day against "permanent inveterate antipathies against particular nations." In uttering this warning, to which he added certain obvious corollaries as to the effect of prejudice, sympathetic as well as antipathetic, upon action, Washington had vividly in mind American conditions, both present and past, of which he had had bitter official experience. His own people had then divided, and was still farther dividing, in sentiment and utterance, upon lines of sympathy for and against Great Britain and France. Impassioned feeling and fervent speech were doing the deadly work he deplored, in setting man against man, and to some extent section against section, upon issues which were at least not purely of American interest. Harmful at any time, such an opposition of misplaced emotions was peculiarly dangerous then, when the still recent union under the Constitution of 1789 had not yet had time to obliterate the colonial habits of thought, to which the common term "American" loomed far less large, and was far less dear, than the local appellations of the several States. This inspired Washington's further very serious and, to use his own word, "affectionate" counsels against the spirit of faction and disunion, which, though not confined to our political community, presented special perils to one but lately organized.

Nor was it only against immediate instances of inveterate national antipathies that Washington uttered his warning. These served him merely as pointed illustrations. He based his counsels, as advice to be sound must ever be based, upon permanent general principles. International relations, he said, were not de-

termined, and should not be determined, by
sympathy, but by justice and by interest. Justice of course first. However onerous and
unsatisfactory, "let existing engagements be
observed in their genuine sense." Beyond this,
" keep constantly in view that 't is folly in one
nation to look for disinterested favors from
another; that it must pay with a portion of
its independence for whatever it may accept
under that character; that by acceptance it
may place itself in the condition of having
given equivalent for nominal favors, and yet
of being reproached with ingratitude for not
giving more."

Here again, in this slightly veiled allusion
to the French alliance, was indicated the intrusion of bias into international relations.
The help extended by France to the American
struggle for independence was indeed real;
but as a favor, though given that coloring, it
was purely nominal. Yet upon it, so regarded,
were based extravagant claims, not only for
American sympathy, but for American active
support in the early days of the French Revolution. Sight was lost of the notorious fact,
that, however disinterested the action of indi-

vidual Frenchmen, the French government, with proper regard to the interests of its own nation, had simply utilized the revolt of the colonies to renew its old struggle with Great Britain under favorable conditions. A large number of Americans, treasuring the then recent occasions of bitter hostility to Great Britain, responded vehemently; another numerous party, alienated by republican excesses in France, and seeing a truer ideal of liberty in British institutions, recoiled with equal vigor. At a moment when every consideration of expediency dictated political detachment, to the intensification of national life, by pruning superfluous activitives and concentrating vital force upon internal consolidation and development, a vast motive power of passion and prejudice was aroused, misdirecting national energy into channels where it not merely ran to waste but corroded the foundations of the Union. On one side and the other, the ideals of national duty and policy became confused with the names of foreign peoples, leading to a bitterness of antagonism that prolonged through a generation the immaturity of the affection uniting the States; maintaining an

internal weakness which manifested itself re-
currently with each fresh cause of variance,
and entailed continued feebleness of external
influence until it disappeared forever in the
agonies of civil war.

It will doubtless be argued that there is now
general recognition that reasoned interest,
controlled by justice, is the true regulator of
state policy. Possibly; but does practice
coincide? Is national calmness or harmony
undisturbed, national force unweakened, by
sympathies and antipathies which, however
otherwise justified, have no proper place in
perturbing international conduct? The fostering of an internal spirit of faction is not the
only evil effect on national judgment that may
arise from extra-national repulsions or attrac-
tions. The immediate evil of disruption, which
then threatened the United States, is indeed
not imminent for political communities of long-
standing consolidation; but even into them
prepossession indulged for or against other
peoples, as such, introduces a motive which
is to national efficiency what a morbid growth
is to the health of the body. The functions
are vitiated, vision impaired, and movement

undecided or misdirected; perhaps both. A tendency arises to seek the solution of difficulties in artificial and sometimes complicated international arrangements, contemplating an indefinite future, instead of in simple national procedure meeting each new situation as it develops, governed by a settled general national policy. The latter course may at times incur the reproach of inconsistency through the inevitable necessity of conforming particular measures to unforeseen emergencies; but it may none the less remain most truly consistent in its fixed regard to a few evident leading conditions for which permanency may be predicated. Washington, a man wise with the wisdom that comes of observation in practical life, phrased this for his countrymen, in the connection already quoted, in the words, "Consulting the natural course of things, forcing nothing;" or, as an American experienced in political campaigning once said to me, "Never contrive an opportunity."

Nothing is more fruitful of that frequent charge of bad faith among nations than the attempt to substitute the artificial for the natural. When subsequent experience shows that interest has been elaborately sacrificed because imperfectly comprehended or wholly misunderstood, popular revulsion ultimately exerts over rulers an influence that is compulsive in proportion to the urgency of the situation. It does not follow from this that a nation, as such, has premeditated bad faith, or wilfully accepts it. Nations are not cynical, though individual statesmen have been. There need be no attempt to justify breach of engagement; but it is a very partial view of facts not to recognize that the greater fault lies with those who made a situation which could not be perpetuated, because contrary to the nature of things. Such action should be accepted as a warning that international arrangements can be regarded as sound only when they conform to substantial conditions, relatively at least permanent. If this caution be observed, national policy may through long periods be as enduring as national characteristics admittedly are. National character abides, though nations under impulse are often inconstant. So may national policy, though on occasion fluctuating, or even vacillating, be really constant; but to be so it must conform to the nature of things, consulting — not resisting — their course.

If this be so as regards general policy, it follows that successive questions, as they arise, should be viewed in their relation to that general policy, which it must be assumed is consciously realized in its broad outlines by the governments of the day. Of such questions the prospective status of Persia and the Persian Gulf now forms one, in the consideration of two or three of the great world powers. In their regard to it, and to the various interests or enterprises centring around it, how far are they guided by the natural tendency of things? How far are they seeking to interject artificial arrangements, forced ambitions? What is to be said, from this point of view, of the proposed activities, the various theories of action, suggested political compromises, that here find their origin? As the phrase "world politics" more and more expresses a reality of these latter days, the more necessary does it become to consider each of the several centres of interest as not separate, but having relations to the whole; as contributory to a general balance of constitution, to the health of which it is essential to work according to nature, not contrary to it.

In the general economy of the world, irrespective of political tenures, present or possible, the Persian Gulf is one terminus of a prospective interoceanic railroad. The track of this, as determined by typographical considerations, will take in great part a course over which, at one period and another of history, commerce between the East and West has travelled. Though itself artificial, it will follow a road so far conforming to the nature of things that it has earned in the past the name of the Highway of Nations. The railroad will be one link, as the Persian Gulf is another, in a chain of communication between East and West, alternative to the all-water route by the Suez Canal and the Red Sea. This new line will have over the one now existing the advantage, which rail travel always has over that by water, of greater specific rapidity. It will therefore serve particularly for the transport of passengers, mails, and lighter freights. On the other hand, for bulk of transport, meaning thereby not merely articles singly of great weight or size, but the aggregate amounts of freight that can be carried in a given time, water will always possess an immense and irreversible advantage over land transport for equal distances. This follows directly from the fact that a railroad is essentially narrow. Even with four tracks, it admits of but two trains proceeding abreast in the same direction; whereas natural water ways as a rule permit ships, individually of greater capacity than any single train, to go forward in numbers practically unlimited. A water route is, as it were, a road with numberless tracks. For these reasons, and on account of the first cost of construction, water transport has a lasting comparative cheapness, which so far as can be foreseen will secure to it forever a commercial superiority over that by land. It is also, for large quantities, much more rapid; for, though a train can carry its proper load faster than a vessel can, the closely restricted number of trains that can proceed at once, as compared to the numerous vessels, enables the latter in a given time, practically simultaneously, to deliver a bulk of material utterly beyond the power of the road.

Commercially, therefore, the railroad system, or systems, and their branches, which shall find their terminus at the Persian Gulf, begin at a great disadvantage towards the Suez route, considered as a line of commercial communication between two seas, or between the two continents, Asia and Europe. This, the broad general result, is, however, only one aspect of the relations to world politics. A railroad, as all know, develops the country through which it passes. This means that it there increases existing interests, and creates new ones. Of these it, and through it its owners, become the fostering and controlling centre. Because of this effect, railroads possess a marked local commercial influence; and commercial influence, especially in these days, and in regions where government is weak or remiss, readily becomes political. It is in measure compelled to political action, to protect its varied interests. Furthermore, railroads serve to expedite not only the movement of commerce but the movement of troops. They have therefore military significance, as well as commercial and political. This is a commonplace, upon which it is needless to insist beyond recalling that it inheres in all railroads as such, and therefore in the one under consideration. Finally, while all parts of a commercial route, by land or by sea, have a certain value, supreme importance is accumulated at the termini, the points of arrival or of departure. The operations of commerce,— receipt, distribution, or transshipment, — are there multiplied many fold. This concentration makes them singularly the objects of forcible interference, and consequently attributes to them an importance which is military or naval, according to the locality. This at present is the particular bearing of the Persian Gulf upon world politics. It is closely analogous to that of Port Arthur, which has preceded it so shortly as not yet to be fairly out of sight, as a matter of international heartburnings. Upon the control of it will rest the functioning of the prospective railroad itself, regarded either as a through line of communication, or as a maintainer of local industries by the access it affords them to wider markets. Not only the prosperity of the railroad itself is at stake. The commercial interests that depend upon it, those of the country through which it runs and to which it immediately ministers, and those of many other regions, as producers or consumers, are involved in the political and military status of the Persian Gulf.

Whose affair then is this, intrinsically so important? Not that of all the world, for though all the world may be interested, more or less, directly or indirectly, it by no means follows that it is everybody's particular responsibility. By established rule and justice, the determination belongs primarily to those immediately on the spot, in actual possession. Unhappily, the powers that border the Persian Gulf, Persia itself, Turkey, and some minor Arabian communities, are unable to give either the commercial or the military security that the situation will require. Under their tutelage alone, without stronger foundations underlying, stability cannot be maintained, either by equilibrium or by predominance. In such circumstances, and when occasion arises, the responsibility naturally devolves, as for other derelicts of fortune, upon the next of kin, the nearest in place or interest. If they, too, fail, then the more remotely concerned derive both claim and duty. The general welfare of the world, as that of particular communities, will be most surely advanced by each one doing that which he finds to his hand to do, whether by direct charge received from due authority, or by inheritance, or from the mere fact of neighborhood, which has given to the word "neighbor" that consecrated association, with the sound of which we are all familiar, though we too narrowly conceive the range of its privilege and its duty.

From the fact of propinquity, of geographical nearness, or of direct political interest, it is easy to see that Great Britain and Russia are the two States which from existing circumstances are most immediately and deeply concerned; nor, when the several circumstances are closely analyzed and duly weighed, does there to my mind seem room to doubt that to the former falls first to say whether she will discharge the duty, or let it go to another. Let there be here interposed, however, the word of caution, before quoted, concerning the natural course of things, lest I should seem fairly chargeable with the disposition, unwise as well as unjust, to favor needless or premature intervention. It may well to-day be a duty not to do that which to-morrow will find incumbent. Opportunity is not to be created, but to be awaited till it appear in the form of necessity, or at the least of clear and justifiable expediency. Consulting the natural order of things, forcing nothing, means at least invincible patience as well as sleepless vigilance; and vigilance includes necessarily readiness, for he only is truly awake who is careful to prepare.

I have said that an analysis of the circumstances shows that Great Britain, in the evident failure of Turkey and Persia, is the nation first — that is, most — concerned. She is so not only in her own right and that of her own people, but in the yet more binding one of imperial obligation to a great and politically helpless ward of the Empire; to India and its teeming population. In her own right and duty she is, as regards the establishment and maintenance of order, in actual possession, having discharged this office to the Gulf for several generations. Doubtless, here as in Egypt, now that the constructive work has been done, she might find others who would willingly relieve her of the burden of maintenance; but as regards such transfer, the decision of acceptance would rest, by general custom, with the present possessor. To her the question is one not merely of convenience, but of duty, arising from and closely involved with existing conditions, which are the more imperative because they are plants of mature growth, with roots deep struck and closely intertwined in the soil of a past history.

These conditions are doubtless manifold, but in last analysis they are substantially three. First, her security in India, which would be materially affected by an adverse change in political control of the Gulf; secondly, the safety of the great sea route, commercial and military, to India and the farther East, on which British shipping is still actually the chief traveller, though with a notable comparative diminution that demands national attention; and, thirdly, the economic and commercial welfare of India, which can act politically only through the Empire, a dependence which greatly enhances obligation. The control of the Persian Gulf by a foreign State of considerable naval potentiality, a "fleet in being" there, based upon a strong military port, would reproduce the relations of Cadiz, Gibraltar, and Malta to the Mediterranean. It would flank all the routes to the farther East, to India, and to Australia, the last two actually internal to the Empire, regarded as a political system; and although at present Great Britain unquestionably could check such a fleet, so placed, by a division of her own, it might well require a detachment large enough to affect seriously the general strength of her naval position. On the other hand, India, considered in regard to her particular necessities, apart from the general interests of the Empire, may justly demand that there be secured to her untrammelled intercourse with Mesopotamia and Persia. She has a fair claim also to any incidental advantage attendant upon the through land communication that can be assured by political foresight, obtaining a position favorable to the negotiations of the future. It is notorious, for instance, that most nations, and Russia pre-eminently, adopt a highly protective or exclusive policy towards foreign industries. Applied to what is now Persia, this would be a direct injury to India, which, even under the present backward conditions of the inhabitants and of communications, carries on a large part of the Persian trade, as might naturally be expected from the nearness of the two countries. The same is doubtless true of her relations with Mesopotamia, though the absence of reliable customs returns prevents positive statements. For securing these natural rights of India, British naval predominance in the Gulf, unfettered by bases there belonging to possibly hostile foreign powers, would be a political factor of considerable influence; but it is incompatible with the establishment of foreign arsenals.

Further, purely naval control is for this purpose a very imperfect instrument, unless supported and reinforced by the shores on which it acts. It is necessary therefore to attach the inhabitants to the same interests by the extension and consolidation of commercial relations, the promotion of which consequently should be the aim of the government. The acquisition of territory is one thing, which may properly be rejected as probably inexpedient; and certainly unjust when not imperative. It is quite another matter to secure popular confidence and support by mutual usefulness. Whatever the merits of free trade as a system, suited to these or those national circumstances, it probably carries with it a defect of its qualities in inducing too great apathy towards the exertion of governmental action in trade matters. Non-interference, laissez-faire, may easily degenerate from a conservative principle to an indolent attitude of mind, and then it is politically vicious. The universal existence and the nature of a consular service testify to the close relationship between trade and government, a relationship that is in some measure at least one of mutual dependence. A certain forecast of the future, a preparation of the way by smoothing of obstacles, a discernment of opportunity, — which is quite different from creating it, — a recognition of the natural course of things at the instant when it may be taken at the flood, these are natural functions of a competent consular body. To it belongs also the establishment of international relations through the medium of personal intercourse, so strongly operative in public matters even in states of European civilization, among statesmen whose business is to look below the surface, and beyond the individual, to the substantial and permanent issues at stake. Much more is it influential among peoples where statesmanship is chiefly a matter of personal interest or bias, consequently short sighted and unstable, and where local confidence and prestige are dominant factors in sustaining policy. There the flag, if illustrated in a well-organized consular service, may well be the forerunner of trade as well as its necessary complement.

At the present time the trade of Persia is divided chiefly between Great Britain and India on the one hand, and Russia on the other. As would be expected from their relative positions, the northern part falls to Russia, the southern to her principal rival in Asia. The one therefore is essentially a land trade, the other maritime. From these respective characteristics, the one naturally induces governmental intervention, to promote the facility of communications, to which the land by its varied and refractory surface presents continual obstacles. The other finds its royal highway of the sea ever clear and open, a condition which ministers to the natural conservatism and acquired principle of non-interference which distinguish Great Britain. By the disposition of all living things to grow, the spheres of the two tend continually to approach. The moment of contact may well be indefinitely distant, but the circumstances which shall attend its arrival are already forming; and when it comes it may be, as now in China, the signal of an antagonism, the result of which will depend upon the facts of political position on the one side or the other. Russia not unnaturally looks to her continuous territory and population, behind the scene of possible contest, as the assurance of her own permanent predominance and eventual exclusive influence. It may be so; but not necessarily until a future so far distant as to be utterly beyond the range of our possible vision, and between which and us lie many chapters of unknowable changes. If confronted by a solid political organism, resting immediately upon commercial interests, and ultimately upon naval control of the Gulf and the armed forces of Great Britain, backed by her colonies and India, it must be long before the northern impulse can overcome the resistance. The physical difficulties of the land route contrasted with the level path of the sea, the narrowness of rail carriage as compared with the broad highway of the ocean, more than compensate for the apparent shorter distance and delusive continuity of the land. The energies of Russia also must long be absorbed by other necessary pre-occupations, notably the far superior importance of developed and consolidated access, by Siberia and Manchuria, to North China seas and the Pacific, the great immediate centres of world interest. There is therefore no need to hasten things in their natural course, but equally there is no justification for neglecting to note and improve them; to quote Washington again, " diffusing and diversifying by gentle means the streams of commerce," which will gradually nurse the future into vigorous life.

Both Persia and China are being swept irresistibly into the general movement of the world, from which they have so long stood apart. Both have a momentous future of uncertain issue, but that of China is evidently more immediately imminent. This is the natural course which things are at present following. Persia has still a time of waiting. The indications also are that Russia, consciously or intuitively, thus reads the conditions. By farsighted sagacity, or through continued yieldings to the successive leadings of the moment, she has now extended her great effort towards sustained communication with ever-open water to the farther East. The Siberian railroad, by which she hopes to assure it, passes through territory that is wholly her own by ancient tenure; while through recent generations she has prepared its security by her steady progress southward in Central Asia and Turkestan. The establishment of orderly government in those regions relieves the flank of the route from predatory dangers, which under the feeble adminstration of Turkey will constitute one of the elements of difficulty for the projected railroad in the Euphrates valley. The Siberian road throughout its whole course is unassailable by any external power, until within a very short distance of the coast terminus. Its military safety being thus absolute, its maintenance, and the development of its carrying power, essential to the Russian position in the farther East, are questions simply of money. Money, however, will be needed in such quantities that the imperative requirements must postpone further effective movement to the southward or westward; for effec-

tive movement means developed communications, consolidated and sustained.   These are
expensive, and in sound policy should not be
attempted on a grand scale in two directions
at the same time ; unless indeed the resources
in money and labor are so great as to justify
their dissemination.   That this is not the case
the notorious condition of the Siberian road
gives reason to believe.

Water communication with the external
world, through an unimpeded seaboard of her
own, is Russia's greatest present want.   For
this object, to what extent would she benefit
commercially by access to the Persian Gulf,
as compared with the China seas?   Putting
out of consideration China itself, with the
nearer shores of the Pacific, as to which the
better situation of Manchuria cannot be questioned, Russia is there much closer also to the
Americas and to the entire Pacific.   Australia
is substantially equidistant from the Persian
Gulf and from Port Arthur; the balance
favoring the latter.   Only Southern Asia and
Africa can be said to be nearer to the Gulf.
Europe and Atlantic America are now reached,
and ever must be reached, commercially, by

Russia, from the Black Sea or the Baltic. From the standpoint of military advantage, a Russian naval division in the Persian Gulf, although unquestionably a menace to the trade route from Suez to the East, would be most ex-centrically placed as regards all Russia's greatest interests. It is for these reasons that I have elsewhere said that the good of Russia presents no motive for Great Britain to concede a position so extremely injurious to herself and her dependencies.

The question of the Persian Gulf, and of South Persia in connection with it, though not yet immediately urgent, is clearly visible upon the horizon of the distant future. It becomes, therefore, and in so far, a matter for present reflection, the guiding principle of which should be its relation to India, and to the farther East. This again is governed by the strategic consideration already presented in the remark that movement, advance, to be effective and sustained, requires communications to be coherent and consolidated. The Russian communication by land, though still inadequately developed, is thus secure, militarily. Throughout its length there exists no near-by point held by an enemy able to interrupt it by a serious blow. The significance of such a condition will be realized forcibly by contrasting it with the military exposure of another great transcontinental line, the Canadian Pacific. In the farther East Great Britain, like Russia, holds an advanced position, chiefly commercial, but consequently military also, the communications of which are by water. These have not, and probably never can have, any military security comparable to that of the Siberian railway. Their safety must depend upon sustained exertion of mobile force, resting upon secure bases, ready for instant and constant action. It is needless to insist upon the difficulty of such a situation; it has been made the subject of recent and abundant comment. But if thus onerous now, all the more reason that the burden should not be increased by the gratuitous step of consenting, upon any terms of treaty, any forced infringement of the natural condition of things, to the establishment of a new source of danger analogous to those already existing in Cadiz, Toulon, the Dardanelles, and so on. Concession in the Persian Gulf, whether by positive formal arrangement, or by simple neglect of the local commercial interests which now underlie political and military control, will imperil Great Britain's naval situation in the farther East, her political position in India, her commercial interests in both, and the imperial tie between herself and Australasia.

So far from yielding here, it appears to me that the signs of the times, as outlined above, point seriously to the advisability of concentrating attention, preparation of the understanding at least, upon that portion of the Suez route to the farther East which lies between Aden and Singapore. In this the Persian Gulf is a very prominent consideration. It is not necessary that material preparation should far forestall imminent necessity; but the preparation of thought which we call recognition, and appreciation, costs the Treasury nothing, and saves it much by the quiet anticipation of contingencies, and provision against them. It tends to prevent inopportune concessions, and the negligences which arise from ignorance of facts, or failure to comprehend their relations to one another. The South African War and the twenty preceding years give recent warn-

ing.   Foreign affairs, as well as military, need
their general staff.   Besides its bearing upon
the Suez route, the Gulf has a very special
relation to the Euphrates valley, and any road
passing through it from the Levant; and this
relation is shared by South Persia, because of
the political effect of its tenure upon the control of the Gulf.   There is here concentrated
therefore commercial and political influence
upon both of the two routes, that by land and
that by water, from the Mediterranean to India
and to the East beyond.   There is no occasion
in the nature of things that Great Britain, either
by concession or compulsion, should share with
another State the control which she now has
here; but in order to retain it she needs not
only to keep the particular protective relations
already established with minor local rulers, but
further to develop and fortify her commercial
interests and political prestige in South Persia
and adjacent Mesopotamia.   This means not
only, nor chiefly, increase of exchange of pro-
ducts.   It means also partnership, public or
private, in the system of communications, analogous in idea, and if need be even in extent,
to Disraeli's purchase of the Suez canal shares.

The attitude of the United States Government towards the projected Panama Canal affords a further suggestive illustration. As towards the farther East, South Persia is in fact the logical next step beyond Egypt; though it does not follow that the connection therewith is to be the same. Correlative to this commercial and political progress, goes the necessity of local provision for naval activity when required. The middle East, if I may adopt a term which I have not seen, will some day need its Malta, as well as its Gibraltar; it does not follow that either will be in the Gulf. Naval force has the quality of mobility which carries with it the privilege of temporary absences; but it needs to find on every scene of operation established bases of refit, of supply, and, in case of disaster, of security. The British Navy should have the facility to concentrate in force, if occasion arise, about Aden, India, and the Gulf.

In summary: Relatively to Europe the farther East is an advanced post of international activities, of very great and immediate importance; but from the military point of view, to which as yet commercial security has to be referred, the question of communications, of the routes of travel, underlies all others and must be kept carefully and predominantly in mind. Russia has her own road, by land, unshared with any other. To the rest of Europe, and to Russia when she chooses, there exists now the sea route by Suez, which is, and probably must remain, supreme to all others. Alternative to it, in part of the way, the future will doubtless bring railways. These, however, on account of the greater cheapness of water carriage, will pretty surely do their principal through business in expediting special transit between the two seas — the Mediterranean and the Indian Ocean. They will in this respect maintain merely an express and fast freight traffic. Between them and the Suez route there will be the perennial conflict between land and water transport, between natural and artificial conditions, in which the victory is likely to rest, as heretofore, with nature's own highway, the sea. But, however that prove, the beginning and the end, the termini, of both routes, land and sea, so far as they compete, will be substantially the same: the Levant Sea, the Straits of Bab-el-Mandeb and the Persian

Gulf. It is too much to ask of international compliancy that Europe should accept the single control of both terminal regions by the same State, especially where no defined claim now exists, as is the case in Levantine Turkey; but equally, where a single government can show a long prescription of useful action, of predominant influence, and of political primacy locally recognized in important quarters, as Great Britain can, there is no reason why she should be expected to abandon these advantages, except as the result of war, if a rival think that result will repay the cost.

There is not to be seen in the nature of things any evidence, or any tendency, which indicates the probability that Great Britain may be forced to yield to compulsion, actual or threatened, concessions of present right which it is inexpedient that she should grant voluntarily. It is upon such probability, conceived to be imminent, that are based proposals of arrangement, or compromise, that I cannot but think excessively artificial, and disregardful of permanent conditions. They surmise, as a necessary postulate, hostile combinations of two or more States, against which,

by a curious intellectual prepossession, no probable counterpoise is discernible. As a matter
of fact, founded upon present territorial positions, there is in the nature of things no real,
no enduring, antagonism concerning the Persian Gulf, except between Great Britain and
Russia. It is not to the interest of any third
State to interfere between these two, or to dis-
turb — much less to destroy — the local balance of power which now exists between them
and can probably be maintained. As regards
its particular interests, the hands of any third
State will be not more, but less, free, should
that balance yield to the decisive predominance
of one of the two throughout the regions involved. Nor can a third State expect to restore equilibrium, if lost, by itself taking the
place of the one that has gone under. It is
only necessary to consider the solidity, extent,
and long standing, of the local control now
wielded by Russia and Great Britain, together
with the land power of the one and the sea
power of the other, to see the hopelessness of
any substitute for either in its own sphere.
The two systems are not dead, but living; not
machines, but organisms; not merely founded,

but rooted, in past history and present conditions. What the rest of the world needs, what world politics requires, is that here, as in Asia immediately to the eastward, there should be political and military equipoise, not predominance. The interests of other States are economical ; freedom of transit and of traffic, the open door. The very problem now troubling nations in the Levant and China is how to establish, — and only afterwards to maintain, — conditions which are already established and have now only to be maintained about the land approaches to the Persian Gulf.

There is therefore, no sound inducement for another State to waste strength here. It can be used better elsewhere. When substantial equilibrium thus exists, a slight effort will suffice to obtain from either party a consideration which in the case of distinct predominance, or exclusive tenure, might require a full display of national power. Doubtless, many in Great Britain, and also in America, are convinced that one third State, the German Empire, is restlessly intent, not only upon economical and maritime development, which is not to be contested by other than economical weapons, but also upon self-assertive aggression with a view to territorial aggrandizement in more than one part of the world; and notably in this particular quarter. A concession has been granted to German capitalists to extend the railway, which now ends at Konieh, to Bagdad, passing through the Euphrates valley. The necessary outlet to this is the Persian Gulf. Such concession, when realized in construction, carries with it a national investment, an economical interest, which, though in private ownership, inevitably entails political interest. It justifies public backing by its own government, in countries where, as in Turkey, private right is secure only when it has national force behind it. It is for this very reason that Great Britain, having already political interest in the Persian Gulf, should encourage British capital to develop communications thence with the interior in Persia and in Mesopotamia, as strengthening her political claim to consideration, and excluding that of possible antagonists. The German road would thus find its terminus in a British system; a not unusual international relation. German enterprise has in anticipation established German political hold upon Asia

Minor and Mesopotamia. As expectation passes into realization Germany will acquire local political importance and influence ; a right, sanctioned by the rules of intercourse with Oriental nations, to have her voice heard in many local matters, as affecting the interests of her subjects who are thus engaged in developing the country.

What effect will this have upon Germany's political and military position, relatively to Russia and Great Britain, which, from nearness or from the commercial ubiquity of their citizens, are also politically interested? Under present conditions Germany, whose nearest port is in the North Sea, has assumed a political burden at a point from which she is far more remote than Russia, and her sea approach to which is before the face of the much greater navy of Great Britain. There is in this nothing to prevent the just assertion of her right, no necessary cause of quarrel, — far from it; but also there is nothing menacing. Germany has simply introduced another factor into a problem as yet unsolved, that of the ultimate political status of several provinces of the Turkish Empire, — Asia Minor, Syria, and Mesopotamia.

As I have elsewhere said, I believe that her appearance there is a step towards a right final solution; that from the necessary common interest of Germany and Great Britain in the Suez route to the farther East, because the commerce of both depends upon its security, the two cannot but work together to secure here a political development which will consolidate their respective naval positions in the Levant.

This seems to me an absolute permanent condition, consistent with a certain amount of mutual jealousy and political wrangling, and with unlimited commercial rivalry, but nevertheless determinative of substantial co-operation. The mass of Russia is so vast, her ambitions so pronounced, and she is so near at hand, that the Suez route needs precisely that kind of protection against her which Russia herself has given to the Siberian road by the regularization of the provinces south of it. Whatever the particular form local administration may ultimately assume, it is imperative upon the Teutonic States to see that their water route to the East is not imperilled by naval stations flanking it, whether in the Levant or in the Persian Gulf. Being themselves far distant, dependent upon naval power simply, it is essential that they constitute a political pre-occupation favorable to themselves in the Asian provinces of Turkey and in Southern Persia. In Egypt and in Aden Great Britain has already done much. Germany, in building a Mesopotamian railway, the continuation of that already working in Asia Minor, contributes to the same end. That Russia looks upon the enterprise with disfavor is a testimony, conscious or unconscious, to its tendency.

These also seem to me permanent considerations. Not less so, having reference to the anxiety felt by some in Great Britain as to the intentions of Germany, is the general situation of the latter in European politics. There is certainly an impression in America, which I share, that Great Britain for various reasons has been tending to lose ground in economical and commercial matters. Whether this be a passing phase, or a symptom of more serious trouble, time must show. Should it prove permanent, and Germany at the same time gain upon her continuously, as for some years past she has been doing, the relative positions of the two as sea powers may be seriously modified. The danger appears to exist; and if so the watchmen of the British press should cry aloud and spare not until all classes of their community realize it in its fundamental significance. Military precautions, and the conditions upon which they rest, have been the main motive of this paper; but these, while they have their own great and peremptory importance, cannot in our day, from the point of view of instructed statesmanship, office-holding or other, be considered as primary. War has ceased to be the natural, or even normal, condition of nations, and military considerations are simply accessory and subordinate to the other greater interests, economical and commercial, which they assure and so subserve. In this article itself, turning as it does on military discussion, the starting point and foundation is the necessity to secure commerce, by political measures conducive to military, or naval, strength. This order is that of actual relative importance to the nation of the three elements — commercial, political, military.

It is evident, however, that these primary matters, although they underlie this argument, are otherwise outside it. For the rest, as regards the general military strength, and in particular the sea power, of the two countries, nothing can overthrow the one permanent advantage that Great Britain enjoys in being insular. Germany, should she realize her utmost ambitions, even expanding to the Mediterranean, must remain a continental State, in immediate contact with powerful rivals. Historically, no nation hitherto has been able under such conditions to establish a supreme sea power. Of this France is the historical example. On the other hand, regarded in herself alone, apart from rivals, Germany cannot, as the United States could not, exert the intense internal effort now required for political consolidation and economical development coincidently with an equal expansive effort. The one may succeed the other, as in our case and in that of Great Britain, where the expansion of the eighteenth century followed and depended on the unifying action of the seventeenth; but, until internal coherence is secured, external expansion cannot adequately progress. One weakens the other. Though correlative, they are not co-operative.

The ambition of Germany so to develop her fleet as to secure commercial transit of the North Sea, which washes her entire maritime frontier, is a national aspiration in itself deserving of entire sympathy.   Towards all other States except Great Britain it is within the compass of reasonable expectation.   As towards Great Britain it is, under present economical conditions, impossible ; for Great Britain, being insular, must maintain continuously supreme the navy upon which her all depends, and moreover, as I pointed out in a recent paper, by geographical position she lies across and flanks every sea route by which Germany reaches the outer world.   This condition is permanent, removable only by the friendship or destruction of the British power.   Of the two the friendship will be the cheaper and more efficacious; for it is needed not in home waters only but in those distant regions which we have been considering.   The naval power of Great Britain is just as real a factor in the future of Germany in the distant East as every thinking American must recognize it to be in our own external policy.   That such a force should be paid for, and must necessarily be maintained, by another people, whose every interest will prompt them to use it in the general lines of our own advantage, is a political consideration as valuable as it is essentially permanent. In the matter of exertion of force it accords absolutely with the nature of things. As for economical rivalry, let it be confined to its own methods, eschewing force.

In saying these things I may seem to ignore the bitter temper, openly and even outrageously shown by the German people towards Great Britain in these last three years. I do not forget it. Human nature being what it is, the dangerous effect of such conditions upon international relations is undeniable. It is ever present to my reflections upon the political future. The exhibition is utterly deplorable, for it can serve no good end, and if it continue will prevent a co-operation among the three Teutonic States which all need, but Germany most of all; for the respective external interests of the United States and Great Britain — together with Japan — have so much in common, and so little that is antagonistic, that substantial, though informal, co-operation is inevitable.

This hostility constitutes an element in the political situation which should be taken into account, and carefully watched. Nevertheless, the permanent conditions, above summarized, will through a future beyond our possible present foresight retain Germany in a position of naval numerical inferiority to Great Britain, as regards both mobile force and the essential naval stations which the latter has acquired during two centuries of maritime activity. These conditions, by their inevitable logic, ought ultimately to overcome a sentiment which has no good ground for existence, and which betrays the national interest. Should it, however, endure, the permanent facts are too strong for it to do more than dash harmlessly against them. Awaiting either event, may not the people of Great Britain on their part, without relaxing vigilance or ignoring truths, accept Washington's warning, which we Americans at least have by no means outgrown, against "permanent inveterate antipathies against particular nations." They have cause for anger; but anger disturbs the judgment, and I think in some measure is doing so in this instance. This particular antipathy is yet young, let it not harden into maturity. In the great political questions which for some time to come will concentrate the external regard of nations and statesmen, the natural desires of Russia, reasonable and unreasonable, are contrary to those of Germany as well as of Great Britain. It is to her clear interest that they remain alienated. Such conditions should on the one hand prompt an earnest effort for a balanced and conciliatory adjustment on all sides; but on the other, their essential permanence, if it be as I think, demands a recognition which would show itself in the extrusion of everything resembling passion, and in the settlement of national purpose on the firm ground of essential facts, instead of the uncertain foundation of any artificial agreement which contravenes them.

THE MILITARY RULE OF
OBEDIENCE

THE MILITARY RULE OF OBEDIENCE

January, 1902.

THE military duty of obedience may be regarded either as a rule or a principle, for
it is both. The rule derives from the principle.
It is the principle defined in precise and man-
datory terms, as a law is the expression of the
general will of the community, formulated by
the Legislature for the governance and control
of individuals. The difficulty of such formulation, however, as that of definition generally, is
well known, and has found proverbial recognition in phrases indicating that statutes, even
when framed with great care by experienced
hands, are very liable to offer loop-holes through
which the observance of them may be escaped.
It is no less difficult to define the military rule of
obedience, without on the one hand constitut-
ing fetters, which would neutralize intelligence
and palsy individuality in a sphere and at in-

stants where both are pre-eminently needed, or, on the other hand, permitting a license which in practice would degenerate into anarchy. It is not a sufficient solution to so knotty and dangerous a question to damn obedience to orders, as a rugged veteran will occasionally be heard to suggest; while, on the other extreme, the saying of that eminent disciplinarian, Lord St. Vincent, "The whole of discipline is contained in the word 'obedience,'" though safer in practice, is perhaps too absolute in its assertion.

The matter at stake is too intricate for such Gordian solutions. It is also too important at once to the individual officer and to the nation, the conduct of whose armed forces may at critical moments depend upon a correct understanding. In many instances, perhaps in the large majority, the propriety of literal obedience is plainly evident; in a few the inexpediency, folly, or impossibility of such compliance is for obvious reasons equally clear; but there nevertheless remain a number of cases, not merely possible, but copiously exemplified by history, which present serious difficulty. In these an officer finds himself confronted with conditions that make a large demand upon his moral courage as well as upon his judgment. His judgment then can be safely guided, and his resolution supported, only by a mastery of principles. No mere rule will here suffice. Military obedience when in subordinate post, and military initiative when in independent command, untrammelled by orders and free to follow the guidance of one's own judgment, are both governed by principles, the appreciation of which is the only sure light to one's footsteps. To them recurrence must be had in doubtful positions, where precise precedent and formal definition are wanting; in short, when rules, however good in general use, fail to apply. It does not hence follow that rules, terse and positive embodiments of principles, such as that of obedience, are mostly useless because essentially narrow and unelastic. That all rules have exceptions is proverbial; and military rules are probably more liable to exceptions than most others, because of the emergency that characterizes war and the vast variety of situations to which a rule has to be adapted. No one proposes on these accounts to disregard rules utterly. It is evident, however, that an officer who undertakes to violate the fundamental rule of obedience, upon the strict observance of which depends in general the success of combined operations, and who substitutes his own initiative for the directions of his superior, assumes a risk which urgently imposes a comprehension of the principles, upon which respectively rest both the rule of obedience and the rules of war.

It may be asserted, as perhaps the most tenable general definition of the principle upon which the rule of obedience rests, that the spirit of obedience, as distinguished from its letter, consists in faithfully forwarding the general object to which the officer's particular command is contributing. This finds expression in the well-known directive maxim, " March to the sound of the guns."   In doubtful cases, however, — and by doubtful I mean cases where action other than that prescribed in the orders seems expedient, — liberty of judgment is conditioned by the officer's acquaintance with the plans of his superior.   If his knowledge is imperfect, or altogether lacking, the doing that which at the moment seems wise to himself may be to defeat a much more important object, or to dissolve the bonds of a combined movement to which his co-operation is essential. If, under such circumstances of ignorance, resting only upon his own sagacity or surmises, he errs either in his reading of his commander's general purpose, or in his decision as to his own action, and through such error disobeys, he cannot complain if he receive censure or punishment. He has violated a recognized rule without adequate reason. The rectitude of his intentions may clear him of moral blame, though not necessarily even so; for the duty of obedience is not merely military, but moral. It is not an arbitrary rule, but one essential and fundamental; the expression of a principle without which military organization would go to pieces, and military success be impossible. Consequently, even where the individual purpose may be demonstrably honest, not wilful, blame adheres and punishment may follow, according to the measure of the delinquency, though that be due to nothing worse than personal incompetency. Does this seem hard measure? It may be replied, in what pursuit is this not so? What is the profession, physician, lawyer, or Wall Street, in which a transgression of instructions by an inferior, or a departure from recognized methods, when not justified by the conditions, escapes punishment, either at the hand of events or of his employer? Is " I thought so," or " I did my best," accepted there as an excuse for disobedience?

In the question of military obedience there is therefore involved both a rule and a principle. In dealing with the matter I shall have to consider both, but I have advisedly chosen the rule for the heading of this article; for, as I have said before, the rule has the force of a law, a law positive in existing enactment, and a law traditional in the settled practice of the military professions, as well as in numerous precedents established by competent authorities. To go behind a law to the principle underlying it, to recognize a higher law than the law explicit, is a very delicate matter for a man in any position; and it is therefore the rule of obedience, rather than the general principle upon which it rests, that most closely touches an officer in military responsibility. Under what conditions is it permissible to disregard orders, or, even more positively, to act contrary to them? What is the real test of propriety, which differentiates one act of disobedience from another of the same apparent character? Is one's own sense of right, one's own good intention, the justifying factor? What judge, however, in such a case is competent to penetrate through the faulty act, if such it be, to the hidden good purpose of the heart? What claim have military men to exemption from the general rule of law, that intention, which cannot be seen, must be inferred from attendant circumstances, which can? If conduct, upon an impartial review of the conditions at the moment of action, is shown to be palpably wrong, by what right can alleged intention, "error of judgment" as it is styled, be invoked to justify an offender? Is there no such thing as malpractice, professionally guilty, though possibly morally innocent? Is professional incompetence, translated into action and injurious to others, never worse than an error of judgment? Mistakes, doubtless, all men are liable to; the fact is proverbial; but the justification of a decision proved by the event to be mistaken rests not upon the intention of the person making it, but upon a judicial review of the circumstances surrounding the decision, which shall prove that, under the conditions known at the moment, it was correct, or at least the most favored by probabilities. If this be true, as I hold it is, in the case even of a man in independent command, much more is the responsibility weighty when action, intrinsically faulty, is taken in disobedience of orders.

The mere enunciation of the queries in the last paragraph will suggest to most that we have here before us no simple question of yea and nay. In fact, no clear-cut absolute reply, no *vade mecum* for pocket use, can be furnished defining just when and how, in all cases, a man is justified in disobedience, nor even when he is justified by blind obedience; although the balance of professional judgment must always incline in favor of the latter alternative. When a doubt arises, as it frequently does, between strict compliance with an order and the disregard of it, in whole or in part, the officer is called upon to decide a question of professional conduct. Personal judgment necessarily enters as a factor, but only one of many; and, to be trusted, it needs to be judgment illuminated by professional knowledge and fortified by reflection. Short of that, it is not a safe counsellor, and has no claim to consideration if cited before a court of final appeal. The officer at the moment should consider himself, as he in fact is, a judge deciding upon a case liable to be called up to a superior court, before which his conclusion has no claim to respect because it is his personal opinion, but only so far as it is supported by the evidence before him. There is, of course, the necessary reservation that the final judgment upon himself, for his professional conduct as involved in his decision, will be rendered upon the facts accessible to him, and not upon those not then to be known, though afterwards apparent.

Unless qualified by these grave considerations, the phrase "error of judgment," so facilely used, is misleading to popular understanding. Not only so; it is pregnant of serious consequences to the issues of war and to individuals influenced by it. It is necessary to realize that some errors of judgment are inexcusable, because inconsistent with recognized standards; and that disobedience of orders is on its face a fault, a disregard of a settled standard, of an established rule, of such general application that upon the person who commits it rests the burden of proving that the circumstances commanded his action. The presumption, in the case of disobedience, is not innocence, but guilt. Mere rule though it be, in its narrow construction and rigid framework, the rule of implicit and entire obedience rests upon reasons so sound that its infringement in action can rarely be condoned, when not thoroughly approved. Nothing can be more disastrous than to trifle with the corner stone, upon which rests the structure of coherent, unified action. The admission into the military mind of anything approaching irreverence for the spirit of military obedience, or levity as regards the letter of the rule in which it is embodied, is the begetter of confusion, and that, in turn, is the forerunner of defeat. To sit loose to this obligation weakens the sense of responsibility, upon the due realization of which rests not merely literal obedience, but intelligent and deserving disobedience in the occasional circumstances which call for that. The recognition of responsibility by the individual, the consciousness that serious regard to it is governing his determinations, is the best moral equipment that a man can have to enable him to sustain the burden of violating instructions, deliberately undertaken upon his own judgment. It is the *mens conscia recti* in a serious problem of action.

The mental equipment is another matter, but it, as well as the moral, are necessary to full professional competency for such occasions. Upon the hypothesis now before us, the rule, absolute in general, seems not to apply. To meet the difficulty with sound discretion, on which to base the defence of his action whatever its issue may prove, the officer will need an adequate realization of all the conditions before him, and a power of appreciating the military situation as thus constituted. This power depends in part upon native aptitude; but it requires also a knowledge of the practice of war, a broad and ripened acquaintance with the principles and precedents controlling the conduct of military operations, which is by no means so widely diffused as may, perhaps, be thought. Without this, disobedience is a hazardous undertaking; but, when so equipped, an officer may with considerable confidence permit himself to depart from the letter of his instructions in order to fulfil their spirit. Confidence, I say deliberately; for in the majority

of such instances he will receive intelligent
and generous consideration.

In such instances it is not just that the propriety of the act should be judged by the
event; and it is not true that it will be, as a
cheap sneer would have it. Success undoubtedly often covers mistakes; for human nature
is on the whole generous, or at least good-
tempered.   It is willing to forgive faults which
it can afford to forget; but failure does not
with any equal certainty entail condemna-
tion, for again mankind is generous, and nowhere more so than in dealing with military
men.   Even though mishap ensue, where an
officer can show preponderant military reasons
for departure from orders, he can anticipate
from his superiors intelligent comprehension
and acquittal, which the public will confirm
on their finding; but, while this is so, let none
be rash enough to anticipate immunity on the
score of error of judgment, when it can be
demonstrated that with the data before him a
man who knew his business would have decided otherwise.

Actions that fly in the face of ascertainable
fact, or of well-settled military principles, are

not to be excused as merely errors of judgment. They are something more, and worse. A man is just as much responsible for an error of judgment which results from his own neglect to inform himself, or his lack of professional knowledge, as he is for any other misdoing. What is amiss here is not judgment, but conduct. Such errors when they take shape in action, whether of commission or omission, are misconduct. They have a standing, as acts, external to and independent of the person committing them, just as murder has a standing as a crime quite independent of its association with the individual criminal. As killing is not always murder, but depends for its character upon the attendant circumstances, so a particular unfortunate military movement is not always misconduct. Circumstances may be proved to justify it. In neither case, however, is it the judgment of the person concerned that determines conduct to have been good or bad. It is the circumstances, passed upon by judges other than himself, and referred to recognized standards. Personal defects may be considered in extenuation, or they may not; their title to indulgence is small where they are due to personal fault or neglect, present or in the past, or to professional incompetency.

If so much as is here claimed be allowed to the military duty of obedience, it is desirable to pass in review the considerations from which such weighty obligations are supposed to derive. Tradition and acceptance, in most men irreflective, have built up an imposing fabric of power, cemented by the habit of rigid, and in the last resort of even blind, submission to superior authority, which, in exhibition and exercise, is directly and immediately personal, though legal in derivation. It will be useful to test the foundations upon which this structure rests, and the necessity, in order to maintain it, of a moral code so foreign to the customary personal independence of the general citizen. Or, if a more vital simile be desired for an organization so instinct with life and regulated movement as a well-constituted military body, let us seek the root, the energizing power of which has evolved, developed, and continues to quicken, military efficiency in all its ramifications, whether in administrative methods or in the principles governing the conduct of war in open campaign.   What we here possess we have through tradition.   Can it give an account of itself?

The value of tradition to the social body is immense.   The veneration for practices, or for authority, consecrated by long acceptance, has a reserve of strength which cannot be speedily obtained by any novel device.   Respect for the old customs is planted deep in the hearts, as well as in the intelligence, of all inheritors of English-speaking polity.   From the very reason of this profound influence over men, traditions need from time to time to be brought to the touchstone, by reference to principle, in order to know whether they are still accordant with the ideas in which their origin is found ; or whether, the ideas themselves being already outgrown, the tradition no longer represents a living present, but only a dead past.   Is the duty of military obedience in either of these cases?   Does the tradition, set forth by the rule, still embody the essential spirit of the principle once involved?   Is the principle itself still alive and applicable as of old?

The question is far from needless, for the contest between the letter and the spirit is constant here, as in many spheres of action.

I am inclined to believe that on shore, among
soldiers, the letter has tended to have the up-
per hand, and with seamen the spirit, due probably to the more frequent removal of the latter
from the presence of an immediate superior,
throwing them thus upon their own initiative.
Naval biography and history, and military history as far as my limited reading goes, seem to
support this opinion. No man wrestled with
the question more vigorously than Nelson;
none found greater exasperation than he did
in the too often successful opposition of the
letter to the demands of his impetuous spirit
for co-operation, addressed to men over whom
he had not immediate control; none was more
generous in his attitude to subordinates who
overrode or overpassed his own orders, provided he saw in their acts the intelligent and
honest will to forward his purposes. Obedience he certainly required; but he recognized
that, given a capable and zealous man, better
work would usually be had by permitting a
certain elasticity of initiative, provided it was
accompanied by accurate knowledge of his
general wishes. These he was always most
careful to impart; in nothing was he more

precise or particular. If he allowed large liberty in the letter, he expected close observance
of, nay, rather, participation in, the spirit of his
ideas. He was not tolerant of incapacity, nor
would he for a moment bear wilful disregard of
his plans. When considerations of high policy
entertained by himself were crossed by Sidney
Smith, his language became peremptory. "*As
this is in strict opposition to my opinion*, which
is *never to suffer any one individual Frenchman
to quit Egypt, I strictly charge and command
you* never to give any French ship or man leave
to quit Egypt." The italics are his own; and
he adds again, as though distrustful still: "You
are to put my orders in force, not on any pre-
tence to permit a single Frenchman to leave
Egypt." The severity of the tone sufficiently
proves his disposition to enforce the strictest
rule, where necessary to control individuals;
but a more liberal reliance upon principle, in
preference to rule, was his habit. None, it
may be added, illustrated more copiously than
he, when a junior, the obedience of the spirit
and the disobedience of the letter. His practice was in this consistent in all stages of his
career. Unfortunately, the example may tempt

smaller men to follow where their heads are not steady enough to keep their feet.

Of course, thinking and feeling thus, he gave frequent expression to his views, and these, coming from a man of his military genius, are often very illuminative. There is one such that is singularly applicable to our present purpose, of searching for the underlying principle which governs the duty and observance of obedience, and determines its absolute necessity to all military action. " I find few think as I do, but to obey orders is all perfection. What would my superiors direct, did they know what is passing under my nose? To serve my King and to destroy the French I consider as the great order of all, from which little ones spring, and if one of these little ones militate against it, I go back to obey the great order."

Carefully analyzed, there is much that is instructive in these words. First of all, it will be observed that the obedience commended is that of the spirit, compliant with general known views. Again, justification of local disobedience also rests upon this compliance with the spirit, applied to the attendant circumstances.

This tacitly admits, of course, that the circumstances must be adequate in order to justify disobedience. It is, however, deeply significant and monitory that the particular sentences quoted were elicited by censure from the Admiralty for disobedience, in the only instance, among many similar liberties of action, in which Nelson failed to establish that circumstances did warrant, or rather did require, him to traverse his instructions. Even he, in the very height of his glory, with reputation, capacity, and zeal, all established beyond question, could not trifle with literal obedience, on the strength of his own judgment, where, upon a calm review of all the facts, the circumstances failed to justify him. He himself, in the exasperation of self-vindication, fell into the facile perversion of thought, concerning error of judgment. " I am so confident of *the uprightness of my intention*, that, with all respect, I submit myself to the judgment of my superiors." "Although a military tribunal may think me criminal, the world will approve my conduct."

What Nelson here meant by "the world" may be doubtful; but it is impossible that the

verdict of history to-day will not affirm the
propriety of the Admiralty's rebuke a century
ago.   The facts, briefly stated, were these.
The Commander-in-Chief of the whole Mediterranean had sent orders to Nelson, his subordinate, to detach a certain part of his force
from Naples to Minorca, which he considered
endangered.   Nelson, anticipating the case,
had argued, to quote his own words, "Should
such an order come, it would be a cause for
some consideration whether Minorca is to be
risked, or the two kingdoms of Naples and
Sicily.   I rather think my decision would be
to risk the former;" and he deliberately disobeyed, resting on this opinion of his own.
His error, however induced, is clear enough.
The Commander-in-Chief was charged with
the safety of the whole field, Naples as well as
Minorca, with many other cases needless to
specify.   It was his business, and his responsibility, to co-ordinate all in a general plan of
offence and defence; in order to carry out
which he had need to count upon the certain
movement of all parts of his command in obedience to his directions.   Refusal in any one
part might throw all out of gear.   Nelson's

particular district, was, simply and broadly, Naples and the Eastern Mediterranean. Within these limits he had full discretion, subject to the general orders of his superior, and his information as to his policy; but when he undertook to act upon his own estimate of the relative value of Minorca and Naples, he went outside the trust and the powers committed to him, and invaded the province which belonged to the Commander-in-Chief alone. His erroneous judgment, or as he styles it, "The uprightness of my intentions," being translated into overt act, became misconduct, and as such was censured by the Admiralty. "Their Lordships do not see sufficient reason to justify your having disobeyed the orders you had received from your commanding officer, or having left Minorca exposed to the risk of being attacked without having any naval force to protect it."

It is perhaps expedient to observe, as tending to confirm a general truth which cannot be too seriously insisted upon, that this unwarrantable action was something more than a breach of necessary discipline, by a man of too assured position and importance to be summarily treated, and who therefore should have been doubly careful of the strict propriety of his course. It was also most unfair to the Commander-in-Chief, in its possible consequences. In case of mishap, the public, less clear-sighted ordinarily than the administration, because more easily moved by appearances, would have sought the first victim of its displeasure in the superior, who had not the same support of past brilliant achievement to fall back on that Nelson had. Nor can it, I think, upon a more detailed examination of the circumstances than is here expedient, be doubted that very serious national disaster was possible, though actually no harm resulted from this breach of discipline.

A previous instance of disobedience on the part of a junior admiral, less than three years before, met with very different measure. Lord St. Vincent, then Sir John Jervis, commanded the British fleet in the Mediterranean in 1796. Scarcity of provisions compelled him to order one of his lieutenants, Rear-Admiral Mann, to take half a dozen ships-of-the-line to Gibraltar, there to fill up, and to rejoin him in Corsica as soon as possible. On his way down, about

October 1, Mann met and was chased by a Spanish fleet of nineteen sail, on their way to Toulon to join the French navy there; Spain having very lately declared war. He escaped, and reached Gibraltar; but on arrival there called a council of war, and upon its advice determined not to carry out his orders to rejoin Jervis. Instead, dominated by the fear of possible consequences, which governed his judgment, he took his division to England. An error of judgment? Yes, according to the common phrase, which the present writer accepted from unchallenged tradition, until forced by reflection to recognize that "error of judgment" was being invoked to cover many acts, very different in their military character.

Mark the result. Because the junction of the Spanish navy to the French gravely imperilled Jervis with fifteen ships in Corsica, Mann judged expedient to leave him in the lurch, instead of obeying his orders and taking back the seven he had with him. Jervis, in perplexed uncertainty, hung on till the last moment, diminishing the rations of his men to one-third of the daily allowance, doubting

and wondering, unwilling to depart lest he
should expose Mann's seven, as Mann was exposing his fifteen. He was, besides, confident
that, if the junction were effected in Corsica,
twenty-two ships, such as he would then have,
would " make their way " through the out-
numbering Spaniards " in every direction ; "
that is, " would cut them to pieces." So much
for the opportunity lost, as Jervis judged it;
in which agreed the opinion of Nelson, who
was with him. We have also the sober meas-
ured judgment of Collingwood on the same
occasion. "We waited with the utmost impatience for Admiral Mann, whose junction
at one time seemed absolutely necessary to our
safety." As for Mann, the Admiralty showed
their appreciation of his judgment by steps
which proved that they considered his conduct
at fault. A cutting rebuke was administered.
"Their lordships feel the greatest regret that
you should have been induced to return to
England with the squadron under your orders,
under the circumstances in which you were
placed." "The circumstances" which governed his judgment did not justify his conduct.
He was deprived at once of his command, and

appears never to have been employed afloat again.

Occurring in so high quarters, and being on so large a scale, these instances show more forcibly than usual what the necessity is, what the root, whence spring the principle, the rule, and the duty — all three — of military obedience. Where many wills have to act to one end, unity of effort, effective co-operation, needs not only to exist, but to be guaranteed by the strongest possible sanctions. The many wills need to become one will; the many persons, in many quarters, simply the representatives, in the best sense, of the one person, in whom the united action of the whole finds source and energy. Lord St. Vincent's maxim, " The whole of discipline is contained in the one word ' obedience,' " may be correctly paraphrased, " The whole of military action is contained in the one word 'unity.' " Obedience and unity are only different manifestations of the same principle. The one is the principle in will, the other in act. The one characterizes the conduct of persons, the other the conduct of operations. Obedience ensures that the members of the military body, often far apart,

will obey the one commander with the accuracy
and vigor with which the muscles of an athlete
obey his will.

In the conduct of war, what is concentration,
the necessity of which is universally granted,
but essential unity? When, for purposes of
the war, concentration yields momentarily to
expansion, then all the movements and dispositions of the forces must be governed by
reference to easy concentration, to unity of
action. The moment this consideration is
violated, unity is sacrificed, and conduct has
become misconduct; nor does it matter, in
justification of a plain violation of principle,
that the misconduct is due to an error of judgment. If circumstances knowable at the tim
justify, judgment has not been at fault; if th
do not, the man should have known bette.
This necessity to keep unity in view is expressed by one of Napoleon's pithy phrases:
" The art of war consists in proper distribu-
tions, to disseminate in order to exist, and to
concentrate in order to fight." Again he says,
" War is a business of positions," and he illus-
trates the maxim by an example of positions
of dissemination, so taken that the scattered

bodies can with certainty and in the briefest period unite at a common centre, in case of threatened attack, or for an intended movement of offence.

In all this there is, of course, much that finds close analogies in civil life, and no doubt much light might be thrown on the rule of military obedience by a comparative examination of other callings. But the peculiarity of war, for which alone the military professions exist, to meet or to avert it, is that men are in the constant presence of power actively and malevolently intent upon injuring them, by any means of surprise or superiority of force that can be contrived. Therefore the need to have every moment in hand, and upon occasion to exert, all the means at one's command, to counteract the enemy, to overthrow his designs, to crush himself, to do so with the utmost speed and certainty, weighs heavier in war than in more tranquil pursuits. War is face to face continually, not with misfortune only but with catastrophe; and that not of gradual approach or partial, but sudden and irremediable.

For these weighty reasons, all available re-

sources to forestall such result, and to destroy
the enemy upon whom it depends, need to be
utilized and put forth in the most effective and
promptest manner.   This means that exertions
in all parts must be instant upon the word of
command, and in unison; united in movement
and united in weight.   Velocity and weight
are the factors of momentum in armed collision as in any other, and both the rapidity and
the force of an intended blow depend upon
unity of impulse and simultaneous impact, in
bodies of men as well as in projectiles.   What
else is the conceded value of movement in
mass than concentrated movement, the weight
of several bodies effectively joined into one?
To frame the plan, to initiate and control the
movement, to give to it direction, combination,
and impulse, to sustain its energy, is the duty
of one man, upon whom in the last analysis
depends the unity of thought and act which
inspires and vivifies the whole; but the transmission of the impulse and energy throughout
the mass, so that the oneness of the head is
realized in the unity of the whole, is ensured
by the military rule of obedience, and by that
only.   Obedience is the cement of the struc-

ture; or, more worthily understood in the spirit, apart from which a word is but dead, it is the life-blood of the organism. In short, the rule of obedience is simply the expression of that one among the military virtues upon which all the others depend, in order that the exertion of their powers may not breed confusion, which is the precursor of disaster, but may accomplish decisive results, approaching perfection in proportion as co-operation has been exact.

ADMIRAL SAMPSON

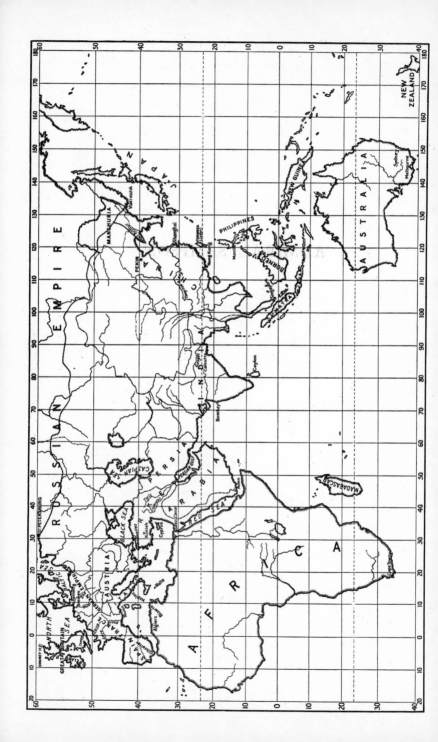

ADMIRAL SAMPSON

May, 1902.

AS a matter of mere retrospect, there can
be few officers now in the navy whose
recollections of the late Admiral Sampson go
back as far as my own. Although a few
months his junior in age, I belonged to the
class at the Naval Academy which was two
years ahead of his; and consequently, at the
time of his entrance, I was able to regard new-
comers with something of that feeling of de-
tached superiority which is apt to characterize
the attitude of older collegians toward fresh-
men. Whatever of distinction between the
two exists in the nature of things is, of course,
emphasized at a military school, where the
want of uniform and difference of carriage
betray at a glance any affectation of composure, with which a stranger may try to con-
ceal the fact that he is in an unaccustomed
position and knows it. At that date — 1857
— the body of midshipmen, as they were then

styled, were organized for purposes of drill
and messing on the same basis as the ship's
company of a naval vessel of the day, in small
groups of sixteen to twenty in number, called
gun's crews.   To each of these was assigned,
in the battery which figured as a ship's deck,
a gun of the type then common in the navy, a
thirty-two pounder; and at the head of each
were two captains, called first and second,
taken from the two older classes.   I was
second captain of the gun to which Sampson
was assigned, and my earliest sight of him was
toward the end of September, when the whole
Academy assembled for the first muster of the
year, the conspicuous incident of the all-round
shakedown with which the annual course began.

It is, perhaps, characteristic of the person-
ality of the man, that even then, under all the
awkward disadvantage of a novice, he made
such an impression upon me that I can at
this moment see his face as I did then, and
as vividly.   Memory plays strange tricks; and
her methods of selecting what she is pleased
to retain defy systematization, or unqualified
approval.   The trivial sticks, the important
escapes; at least we often so estimate its ac-

tion. In this case I do not mean in the least
to convey the idea that I then recognized, consciously, that the person before me was one of
superior intellect or character, marked though
Sampson afterward proved to be in both those
respects. Nevertheless, I do find it noticeable,
in the light of his subsequent career, that he,
and he alone, of all the youths then about me,
has left an abiding remembrance. I had a
hard wrestle with my recollections a few days
ago to recall who was the first captain of that
crew. I got him at last; but memory is ob-
stinate in refusing me the names or faces of
the men who sat on my right and left hand at
mess during the eight following months which
made the academic year of study. Sampson
alone of the whole group has stuck.

Although I did not then, nor for long afterward, analyze the reason for this arrest of attention, which forced memory to take hold and
pigeon-hole a portrait for future reference, I
incline to think that it was due to the unusual
inquisitive interest he showed in all that was
going on. This trait was carried into his subsequent professional life as a whole. It was
the necessary complement to his very excep-

tional intellectual capacity, without which his natural abilities might have been wasted, as have been those of so many other gifted men in all callings. The average raw boy, in his then position of entrance to the Academy, yields passively, and with a certain sense of subjection, to the impulse of those above him. He does what he is told, asks no questions, and gradually learns by familiarity what he has to know and to do. Commonly, too, he acts thus through life. He goes through his round, doing his duty; for, if he learns nothing else, that at least the navy drives thoroughly home, and from that lesson the *personnel* of the service becomes the thoroughly reliable instrument it always has proved on demand. For average results the motive is sufficient. But the desire for personal advancement is stifled by the rule of promotion by seniority; and consequently the only stimulus in peace, to exertion beyond the simple line of duty, is the influence of a lively interest in matters professional for their own sake. This creates initiative and sustains energy, thus becoming a productive force for personal improvement, as well as for naval progress. This Sampson had, and to it he owed

the advance and eminence which constitute
the self-made man. Yet he was entirely without the aggressive self-assertion which is often
the unpleasant accompaniment of those who
realize that they owe their fortunes to themselves. There was in him an inherent modesty and simplicity, through which there
transpired no evidence of consciousness that
he had made himself more than others. In
all my intercourse with him he never gave any
indication of knowing that he was a man of
mark; and as he rested contentedly in the
sense of duty done, for its own sake and its
own interest, so he never sought other approval than his own. He had none of the
tricks of the popularity hunter, and he suffered
for it.

In the very small beginnings of his introduc-
tion to naval life, at our first meeting, Sampson began as he afterwards continued; putting
me through a searching series of questions
concerning the matters around him. He
clearly, if unconsciously, intended not to wait
till knowledge came to him of itself, if he could
compel it to hasten. I should not call him
handsome, as I remember him then, though

the elements of the singular good looks that
he possessed in early manhood were all there
— an unusually fine complexion, delicate, regular features, and brown eyes remarkable both
in shape and color. The smooth, round face
struck me as over small, and the beauty which
in his prime was thoroughly masculine, seemed
then wanting in strength — a singular misread-
ing. He had just about as much — or as little
— carriage and bearing as the ordinary country
lad of his age, emphasized by a loose mixed
suit, ready-made and ill-fitting. He owed,
therefore, nothing to adventitious external circumstances. The figure, which soon after
broadened and gathered erectness and firmness, gave then an impression of slightness
amounting to fragility, which was pathetically
recalled to me by the shrunken aspect noticeable after the Spanish War, when prolonged
frail health and incipient decay had wasted
the vigorous frame I had once known, and
set on him the mark of death's approach. I
remember also that his manner in questioning
was not only interested, but eager, affecting the
play of the face; in this differing from the impression usually conveyed by him in mature

life, which was one of too great quiescence. This was really an evidence of temperamental calmness, of self-composure, not of indifference, for he was susceptible of strong feeling, and at times exhibited it; but commonly his features, though little open to criticism otherwise, were too statuesque and unemotional.

To one with a prophet's eye, the conjunction of the raw country lad who was questioning me with the scene surrounding him would have constituted an artistic epitome of our naval history, past and future. The material of naval war was then on the eve of an epoch of transition, in which he was to play a part so prominent as to associate him continuously with its entire progress. The guns and carriages among which we stood, and the implements with which they were served, differed little in size and nothing in method from those with which the War of 1812 had been fought. There was then being introduced a new class of cannon, resembling the old in type, but exaggerated in size and improved in manufacture, with some scientifically calculated modifications in form, and with new methods of handling. The particular effective feature of these, however, was the throwing of explosive shells instead of solid shot. With them mainly the Civil War was to be fought; but their designer, the most prominent ordnance officer then in the navy, still rejected the project of rifling great guns, as being needless for sea warfare. "Those who mean fighting," he was reported to have said, "will come within smooth-bore range;" an unconscious plagiarism upon Nelson, who was indifferent to improvements in sighting, on the avowed ground that it was better to go so near the enemy that you could not miss. The other considerations which compelled the acceptance of the rifle, — notably sustained velocity and penetrative force, — were then little accounted of; for the armoring of ships was in an uncertain infancy. The turret system, soon to play so great a part, was yet a germ in the thought of its inventor, unknown to the professional world.

It will easily be understood that after our first interview the difference of classes between us prevented any growth of intimacy, beyond the occasional and entirely routine association of the drill ground; and there, as silence was the rule for all except necessary orders, acquaintance could scarcely make further way. We saw little or nothing of each other, save in the most casual manner, up to the time of my graduation in 1859. He remained until 1861, the outbreak of the Civil War, when he graduated in due course; the war not having the effect upon his class, which it did on some that followed, of shortening their time at the Academy in response to the urgent demand of the service for more young officers. His career throughout was in scholarship most distinguished; giving, withal, that assurance of force of character as well as intellectual capacity which led to his long identification with the Academy in after years. First as an assistant, afterwards as the head of one of the scientific departments, ultimately as superintendent, no naval officer has been more broadly associated with it, or made a more marked impression. He declined decisively, however, to entertain a proposal made to him, to remain as permanent head of the department which he successfully administered from time to time. There was much that was tempting in an offer, which would substitute, for the family partings incidental to a naval career, a comfortable fixed home and steady congenial employment; but in speaking of it to me he alleged his unwillingness to be severed from immediate association with the profession of his education and friendships. As it was, his constant returns to the same sphere of duty were, like his other conspicuous employments, one part of the unexpressed tribute, the tribute in act rather than word, which the service paid to his merits. Not that words were wanting; but men spoke them among themselves, rather than to him or to the public. The professional recognition which followed him, and still follows, was largely silent; but I believe it was, and is, as competent and instructed as it is positive and even enthusiastic.

Of this I am, perhaps, the better judge, in that my own personal knowledge of him is chiefly at second hand, not direct. I am rather a witness to general reputation than an eye-witness of conduct or character. Though I knew him well, and met him often, and so had occasion by experience to corroborate the general estimate, we were rarely associated, and never closely. Intimacy never existed between us, and there was no chance for me thus to form that prepossession of esteem which I had ample occasion to note among those who had seen him in active service. Officers who had been under his command afloat spoke of him with a warmth of admiration and confidence, the sincerity of which was too obvious for doubt. To those who, like myself, learned in this way how he was regarded by the men who had been best situated to observe him, there was little surprise at the eminent characteristics shown by him during the late war; nor had there been antecedently any fear whether the Navy Department was exercising sound judgment and discretion in selecting him for the position he held. His very remarkable fitness for particular duties, which had to be discharged on shore, had kept him decidedly below the average in the amount of what is technically rated as " sea-service; " but that which he did left no apprehension among those who saw him that the habit of the student or administrator had swamped the faculties of the sea officer. He was to add another example to the list of those who have proved by their deeds, that the professional capacity of the seaman is at least as much a matter of intelligence as of uninterrupted practice, and that, once acquired, it is very like other habits, easily resumed after intermission, and quickly restored when a little rusty.

Prominent among the aptitudes of the competent commander, however, are certain moral faculties which are not acquired by practice, though they may by it be improved and enlarged; gifts from Nature, who in such matters knows nothing of impartiality. It was upon these traits in Sampson that men seemed instinctively to dwell, and by them chiefly to be impressed. Their estimates were not reached as a matter of analysis, but were received by incidental familiarity and daily observation of the man. As I met his reputation from time to time in conversation with men, in their opinions and anecdotes, as I knew him by what they thought and quoted about him, there formed gradually in my mind a conception of his professional character which the event has proved to be substantially correct. The more naval history and biography are read, the more do they confirm to us the assurance that in successful leaders there are certain essential qualities, the absence of which in a particular man may remain long undetected, like a flaw beneath the surface of metal, but under strain is suddenly revealed, to the disappointment and dismay of those who had hopes of him. No one has phrased this experience better than Lord St. Vincent, in the words, " Responsibility is the test of a man's courage." Not that many men who here fail are not brave enough physically; but that, for those who emerge unbroken from this trial, there remains none severer. It is the extreme proof of endurance, active and passive. A frequent and familiar indication of succumbing under it is the inability to sleep, which has been the prelude of many failures.

It was upon this characteristic, and upon the qualities accessory to it, that there was consensus of opinion in Sampson's case. However differing otherwise in details, all agreed in the conclusion that upon him responsibility sat easily; that anxiety did not overrun the due bounds of reasonable, though watchful, precaution; that he could rest with quiet mind in the certainty that all had been done which reason could prescribe, untroubled by fears of improbable, though not impossible, eventualities. To this is closely allied the very essential power to take necessary risk for adequate ends, a thing almost impossible to a man upon whom responsibility weighs unduly. This was finely, though unconsciously, illustrated in his orders for the blockade of Santiago. "The end to be attained justifies the risk of torpedo attack, and that risk must be taken. The escape of the Spanish squadron at this juncture would be a serious blow to our prestige, and to a speedy end of the war." To one who has listened, as I have, to one of his gallant captains telling, in laughing earnest, the number of torpedo-boats imagination discovered in one of the early nights of the Havana blockade, these words mean more than they will, perhaps, convey to a layman. It is in this danger, in its anxiety even more than in its actuality, — in its moral effect, — that the naval profession recognizes one of the greatest difficulties of a modern blockade. A distinguished British admiral has said that he believed but a small proportion of captains could long endure the nightly strain. Sampson assumed it without hesitation, though not without assiduous precaution, as is shown by the numerous orders issued by him to perfect the methods. The danger was shared by many; the responsibility of the means, which effectually prevented the enemy from coming out by night, and so confusing the movements of our squadron, was his alone.

It is evident that this professional faculty was part of his natural equipment, and it manifested itself in his personal daily life. In conversation, ordinarily, there was nothing more noticeable than a certain impassivity of manner that was readily mistaken for indifference or lack of response. This at times gave offence, particularly in his later years, when bodily weakness imparted lassitude to his speech. But when consulting him on a matter of interest to another, one found that he had carefully followed what was said, giving both thought and sympathy to the discussion; while in matters that primarily concerned himself he was in all outward semblance, and I believe internally, just as quiet and untroubled as about the most trivial external detail. I remember meeting him the day after the monitor " Patapsco " was sunk by a submarine mine off

Charleston, a personal experience which would have made many men nervous as well as careful about torpedoes in after life. With her small reserve of buoyancy, a torpedoed monitor went from under the men on deck with something of the suddenness of the drop of a gallows, and Sampson, who was keeping watch on the turret roof, described his experience as stepping from it into the water. Nevertheless, when I saw him, he was as unaffectedly and without effort imperturbed as though nothing remarkable had occurred. Quite consistent with this observation of my own is the account given of him off Santiago by his flag-captain, Chadwick, in an admirably sympathetic sketch contributed after the admiral's death to the New York *Evening Post.* " He usually had a chair upon the quarter-deck until about ten in the evening, when he turned in and slept soundly, unless called for something important, until six in the morning. His calm, equable temperament carried him through the night without any of the sleeplessness usually associated with the mental strain of great responsibilities."

In his conduct of a war command, however,

there was not to be found any of the lethargy
or sluggishness which might, perhaps, be inferred from this unmoved exterior. Mental
activity and enterprise suffered nothing, but
rather gained, from a composure of spirit which
preserved all his other faculties from derange-
ment, insuring the full utilization of the
abundant intelligence, extensive professional
knowledge, and vivid interest in his work, by
which he was characterized. It is true that
apathy is the defect of this quality of composure, and in military biography has often been
found to accompany it. During the Civil War
there was an amusing anecdote of a certain
commanding officer in a particular incident.
" Was he composed ? " it was asked. " Oh, yes !
he was perfectly composed," was the reply;
" but he had n't the faintest idea of what ought
to be done." Sampson's professional character
was here well balanced. It was only in the
matter of personal ambition, of self-assertion,
or self-vindication, that his reticent calmness
entailed an inaction, which, though dignified,
and preservative of his own self-respect as of
the esteem of his comrades, did not save him
from suffering keenly when he thought himself

unworthily treated. He consulted me on one occasion as to how far it would become him to take action that had been suggested for his benefit. I told him that while I heartily wished him all the good that was at stake, I believed the particular step would be injurious to the navy. He expressed no decision to me then or afterwards; but I thought I read assent in his eyes, and I know that he went no farther in the matter.

The opening acts of a war drama, especially after a long period of peace, are necessarily characterized by a considerable tension of feeling among the actors, which seeks natural relief in immediate action. So big a deed as war calls clamorously for something to be done, and speedily. Probably few appreciate in this light how great was Dewey's privilege in the opportunity, so consonant to his personal qualities, and of which he so admirably availed himself, overriding all consideration of hazards, to strike at once at the enemy's fleet at its anchorage. Upon Sampson fell the more arduous trial of prolonged expectancy, in unavoidable attendance upon the enemy's movements, which he could only by indirection force or control; submitting to the necessity of not attempting to enter a harbor like Santiago, or risking on mine fields the armored ships which were the nation's most important diplomatic asset at that moment. In this he had no choice. The orders of the Government were positive, though his own opinion coincided with them. No man was more fitted by temperament than he to bear this strain, without disturbance of judgment or inconsiderateness of act. The tension which he felt in common with others manifested itself in sustained energy, rising indeed on necessary occasion to impetuosity, but characterized rather by the continuous and increasing stringency of methods adopted to meet a sortie by the enemy. In the strong professional admiration I have felt for his conduct of operations in every respect, as soon as the appearance of the enemy's fleet had really defined the situation, it has been to me a matter of satisfaction that my judgment differed decisively from his own in two preliminary matters: his wish to attack the sea defences of Havana, and the expediency of his movement against Porto Rico, undertaken in the hope that on arrival he would find Cervera there. Soon after the war I criticised the latter step in the pages of *McClure's Magazine*, drawing from him a warm remonstrance on what he considered an inadequate appreciation of his reasons. Whether he or I was right in this is to me immaterial, compared with the fact that it gives me assurance of my own impartiality in the profound admiration I have felt for all his dispositions and actions, without exception that I can recall, from the time he knew the enemy to be on this side.

The methods of the Santiago blockade are now commonly understood, but their precise military merit has scarcely been adequately appreciated. By them, as appears from the Spanish telegrams published since the war, Sampson compelled the enemy to accept battle on the terms they considered most disadvantageous. Many may remember the classical story of the leader who cried to his opponent, " If you be the great commander men say, why don't you come down and fight me ? " and received the pertinent reply, " If you be the general you claim to be, why don't you *make* me come down and fight you ? " This summarizes in effect the credit due to Sampson. On June

26, just a week before the battle, the Spanish
authorities at Madrid and Havana had decided
that the surrender of the squadron in Santiago,
or its destruction there by its own officers,
would be more injurious to their cause than its
destruction in battle, and they held that, by
"choosing a dark night and favorable opportunity while part of the enemy's ships are withdrawn," there was a fair chance of eluding the
United States fleet. Cervera replied that to
go out "at night was more perilous than in
daytime, on account of the hostile ships being
closer inshore." After the war, he explained
at length, in a letter dated October 7, 1898:
"At night the enemy remained in the immediate vicinity of the harbor entrance. They
always had one ship less than a mile distant,
constantly illuminating the entrance; and as
though this were not enough, they had other
smaller vessels still nearer, and steamboats
(launches) close to the headlands of the entrance. Once in a while the latter would exchange musketry fire with our forces. Under
these circumstances it was absolutely impossible to go out at night, because in this narrow
channel, illuminated by a dazzling light, we

could not have followed the channel. But even supposing we had succeeded in going out, before the first ship was outside we should have been seen and covered from the very first with the concentrated fire of the whole squadron." These details will be found to correspond with Sampson's published orders.

The thoroughness of the blockade after Sampson's arrival determined the detention of Cervera in Santiago till our army arrived. To use an expression of one of the American captains, it "put the lid on Cervera's coffin." After the army came, the same measure determined the destruction of the squadron if it attempted to escape; for it decided the time and conditions under which the battle would be fought, when on July 1, the further land defence being considered practically hopeless, a peremptory order to sail was given to Cervera. The forcing of the enemy to action under these disadvantageous conditions was the great decisive feature of the campaign from start to finish.

The skill with which advantage was taken of all the possibilities of the situation was characteristic of Sampson's deliberate painstaking energy. No less characteristic, indicative of the sustained purpose which rises of its own force to impetuosity, when impetuosity is needed, was his urgent repeated telegram to the Department for its sanction to go to Santiago with only two ships, dropping the slower but powerful battle-ship " Indiana," when news was received that Commodore Schley felt it necessary to bring back his squadron to Key West for coal. For once he betrayed impatience at the apparent delay of the Department, although it replied the same day. It was a flash of the fire that burned within him unremittingly, but with regulated fervor; a token of the entire absorption in his duties which was the groundwork of his professional character. Disregardful of all but the necessity of success, he was heedless of personal danger, and daring in professional risk. The mastery which the service had over his interest and affections, united to entire self-mastery in temper and under responsibility, insured his eminence as an officer, which history will unquestionably recognize and affirm.